Ekadashi kathamrutam

Janak R. Jalundhwala

(Gujarati to English) Translated by Rajeshri Dani

"Connect the Vision"™

Nexus Stories Publication

Bhārata

NEXUS STORIES PUBLICATION
Surat, Gujarat, India.

Title – Ekadashi Kathamrutam

First Published by Nexus Stories Publication 2022

ISBN # 978-93-91529-84-0

Publication
Nexus Stories Publication™, Surat (Gujarat), Bhārata
https://nexus-stories. com, +91 87800 80718

Content

Introduction

सर्वार्थसंभावो देहो जनितः पोषित यतः ।

नतयोर्याति निर्वेशं पित्रो मर्त्यः शतायुषा । ।

Shrimad Bhagwat (10/45/5)

Many great men have enlightened the soul to achieve 'Dharma', 'Artha', 'Kama', and 'Moksha'. or even lived up to be a hundred years old. Even those great men cannot repay their parents the debt of life which is given them.

Ekadashi is the eleventh lunar day (tithi) of every fortnight in the lunar month. On this auspicious day of Ekadashi in most Hindu houses some other spiritual activities like fasting, reciting religious stories, reading religious scriptures, bhajans, etc are done with family members. The impact of such activities is miraculous which one can feel only after the experience.

In our house also my late grandmother Leelawati Ratilal Jalundhwala was doing such activities with a group of ladies and even after her death, the legacy was continued for years.

This book is published by my father Janak. R. Jalundhwala in her memory. It contains stories of Ekadashi, religious rituals to follow on that day, and its intellectual importance. With the hope, 'Ekadashi Kathamrutam' will become useful to devotees. Please excuse us if there is any gaffe (mistake).

Jai Shri Krishna.

Forum Gandhi (12th July 2021)

1. Story of Ekadashi Mata / Goddess Ekadashi

Many years ago, in the era of Satyug, there was a very powerful demon. His name was 'Moor' and he was the son of the 'Nadijangh' demon. Moor worshipped Lord Brahma relentlessly for several years and pleased him.

Pleased Lord Brahma told Moor that any wish his heart desired would be granted, he said, "please grant me the blessing, that no Devta shall be able to kill me." Lord Brahma said 'Tathastu' and fulfilled his wish. Moor was already powerful but after receiving blessings from Lord Brahma he became adamant and lordly. He defeated 'Indra, 'The king of all Devtas, and his demigods. He declared himself as 'Indra' and took over his court along with his demon allies. Disappointed by their defeat and helplessness Devtas went to Lord Brahma and narrated what had happened. It was a difficult situation because after giving a boon, Lord Brahma was also unable to kill him, so they all went to Lord Shiva but even he was also unable to help to solve the problem, so they all went to Lord Vishnu. Lord Vishnu was resting in his milk ocean which is Kshirsagar. All Devtas along with Lord Brahma and Lord Shiva stood at the bank of the milk ocean in near-white light and worshiped Lord Vishnu. When he appeared the Devtas presented their problem to him and sought a solution. He promised the Devtas to protect them and kill the Demon. Lord Vishnu went to Chandrawati city where Moor was staying, along with Devtas, and declared war against him, by chanting his Panchjanya Shankh. The war between Devtas and demons started. Devtas fled after some time because they could not cope with Moor. Lord Vishnu continued the battle for a thousand years, but the monster was not defeated.

Lord Vishnu decided to defeat and kill Moor with another technique, so he escaped from Chandrawati and went to the Sinhwati cave in Badrinarayan, which was around 12 yojana (1 yojana is equal to approx. 8 miles) long and it had 164 gates. He introverted all his eleven organs (that has ten senses and one mind) and sat in yoga-Nidra meditation. When Lord Vishnu was meditating, a girl's body appeared from his body and a beam of light from his introverted organs. They both merged and turned into very beautiful, gorgeous, and brave goddesses. She was surrounded by a divine aura and her hands were loaded with weapons. When Moor reached there, he saw that Lord Vishnu was meditating and the beautiful girl was standing nearby. He got attracted to her and proposed marriage. The Goddess had a prompt reply, "I have a vow that I will marry a person who will defeat me in war." Moor, blinded by her beauty, was desperate to marry her, so he accepted the challenge. The goddess was not only brave but also a good warrior. Within a few minutes, she defeats him and kills Moor.

After some time, Lord Vishnu emerged from his meditation and was surprised to see that his enemy was killed. He asked, "who killed this brutal demon?" Goddess replied, "I have killed him. I am born from your powers to kill the evils from the whole world."

Lord Vishnu was highly pleased with her answer. That day was the eleventh day (tithi) of the waning phase / Krishna paksha of Kartik month. So, he named her 'Ekadashi' and asked for blessings.

Goddess Ekadashi replied, "If you are really happy, please give blessings to people who observed my Vrat, keep fast on

Ekadashi day. They should be redeemed from their sins and all their wishes get fulfilled in their life and thereafter. Those who are unable to fast due to illness but perform devotional services too will get rid of their sins and remain happy. You are my master because I am born out of you so give pleasure to me on all my days and my significance should remain always and forever.

Lord Vishnu happily declared that you will be famous by name of ' Bhaktida ' and 'Muktida. ' (that goddess who offers worship and divine Liberty) and who observes fast on Ekadashi day I will fulfill all his wishes. This was the day of origin of Ekadashi which is why this Ekadashi is also known as ' Utapatti Ekadashi.' Lord Vishnu made the other Devtas and sages of Badrinarayan fellow to observe this Vrat and from that day all Devtas or humans follow this, Vrat.

*****

2. The religious significance of Ekadashi

Word Ekadashi is derived from Ekadash. Ekadash means eleven. There are two fortnights (lunar phases) or paksha in each lunar month. One is called Shukla paksha (Sud)/waxing phase and the other is Krishna Paksha (Vad)/waning phase. The 11th day of every fortnight is known as Ekadashi or Agiyaras. That way we have twenty-four Ekadashi in one year.

Every third year there are twenty-six Ekadashis because of one additional month known as Adhik Maas.

Ekadashi Mahatmya

Indian sages have played an important role in elevating Indian culture. They have given thoughts about sin and virtue, heaven and hell. They instructed man to work in a good way, to do good deeds, to chant, to do penance, to fast, etc. That is why in Hinduism the fast on an agiyaras tithi is observed. The day of Ekadashi is dedicated to Lord Vishnu because the origin of the goddess Ekadashi is Lord Vishnu himself. The significance of all Ekadashi through its different stories is written in Purana, (old religious texts) and that is why the religious significance of these Vrat is also very great.

Pushti Marg:

Shrimad Vallabhacharya who established Pushti sampradaya also commanded all Vaishnavas to observe Ekadashi Vrat. He has written in Tatvarthdeep SarvaNirnay Karika-245.

एकादष्युपवासादि कर्तवय वेद्यवर्जितम
तथा कृष्णाष्टमी याषी सप्तमी वेधवर्जिता
अन्यान्यपि तथा कुर्यादुस्तवो यत्र वै हरे: ।

This means One should fast on Ekadashi day without any hesitation, not only that but also on the birthdays of Lord Vishnu's incarnation like Shri Ram- Navami, Shri Janmashtami, Shri Nrisimha chudash, and Shri Vaman-Jayanti. Shri Krishna has exhibited various activities to serve mankind which includes killing demons like Putana, Shatkasur, Trunavat, Bakasur, Dhenukasura, Adhyasur, and KaliNag and giving them moksha (liberty from rebirth). All these activities he did on the day of Ekadashi in Vraj(Gokul) and the message he wanted to convey was that is that if one (soul) wants to reach to God should be able to get free from Dehadyas, i.e. free from all five senses that are, ear, nose, tongue, eye, skin and all five work senses that are hand, leg, mouth, anus, genitals. One should try to be attached more and more to God and try to detach from the material world. One has to constantly remember, Chant, and praise God with the feeling that I belong to the Lord and the Lord belongs to me because God is omnipresent. One should remember God and his activities with devotion.

In pushti sampradaya only Bhagwad seva is sufficient. One who does that is not required to do vrat, fast, constant chanting, etc. But till the time one is not free from the material world and attached with bodily desire (dehadhays) Shri Mahaprabhuji commands   all pushti devotees to follow the rules of Varnashrama, that is laws and duties related to varna/ cast where one has born and stage he lives in

(Four cast Brahmin Kshatriya vaishya and shudra and to all four stages of life brahmacharya ashram, grihastha-ashram, vanaprastha ashram, and sannyasa ashram) as much as possible. Shri Mahaprabhuji has described the significance and spiritual election of each Ekadashi through different stories and incidents.

Maryada path

Maryada path believes that fasting, chanting, penance, sacred bath, bhajans, puja, yagna, etc. whatever is done on the day of Ekadashi never go waste. At the time of death, the soul of such a person is not taken away by agents of Yamraj known as Yamdtutas but by agents of Lord Vishnu, known as Parshada, and placed in Vaikuntha Dham.

Ekadashi Vrat for dead people. (Mrit Atma)

Knowingly or unknowingly human beings commit many sins from birth to death. When someone dies, his family and relatives always wish that his soul should be free from those sins and obtain Vaikuntha Dham. In Sanatan, Dharma Ekadashi holds great importance. It is considered the king of all Vrats and Lord Vishnu also admires Ekadashi vrat. If chanting, penance, and other virtues, including Ekadashi, are done with a lot of faith and love over a long period it becomes beneficiary for the upliftment of departed souls. That is why the family of departed souls observes Ekadashi fast for one year after the death of the deceased so that he attains peace, bliss, and liberation, the sins of the deceased may be eradicated, attain Vaikuntha Dham, and reborn as a human.

*****

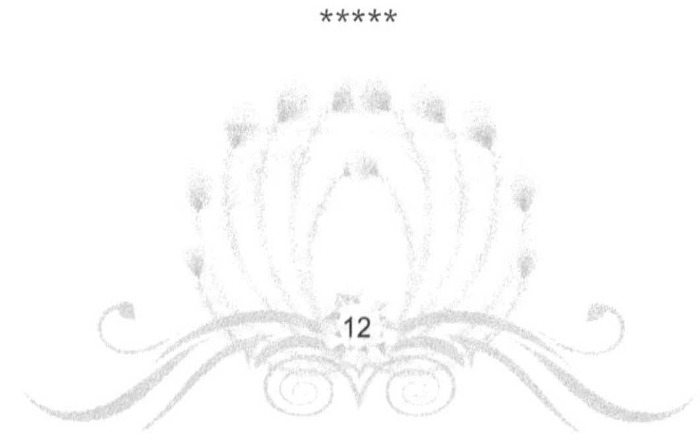

3. Ekadashi Vrat

Ekadashi vrat rituals are performed on the eleventh day of each fortnight. Each day is called ' tithi '. For e.g.: the first day is ekam tithi, the second day is beej tithi, etc.

<u>Ekadashi day</u>

According to the Vedic Hindu calculation each tithi begins at sunrise of that day and lasts till the next sunrise. Whereas 'Skanda Purana' shows different calculations for Ekadashi day. According to it, if the day of Ekadashi starts ninety-six minutes before sunrise, then Ekadashi is considered a pure Ekadashi, but if the Ekadashi starts less than ninety-six minutes before sunrise that Ekadashi is considered impure.

According to Garuda Purana, Bhavishya Purana by Kanva rishi, Shree Hari-Bhakti Vilas, and Vaishnav Smriti if Ekadashi tithi is not seamless then it continues for two days. The first one is known as *'Smarth Ekadashi'* and the other as *'Vaishnav Ekadashi.'* Vaishnava devotees have to keep Vrat on the second day.

In a month where Ekadashi is celebrated along with the previous tithi i.e., Dasham, the demons are nearby. For that reason, one should not fast on such Ekadashi tithi. It is said that Gandhari had observed such Ekadashi Vrat, as a result, her hundred sons Perished in her lifetime.

Many times, one gets confused about when to fast because of repetitive tithi and we find different opinions in different texts. A solution to this is given as one should fast on the twelfth tithi, i.e. dwadashi or Baras day. When Ekadashi, Dwadashi, and teras all 3 tithis are on the same day it is known as 'Triyodashi or Trisarva'. Ekadashi fasting can be done on Triyodashi day.

(Chapter 125 of Garuda Purana in brief)

Types of Vrat

Daily Vrat - chanting, bhajan, Puja any activity which is performed every day.

Vrat with intention - when Vrat is observed with some intentions of Goodwill.

Desire / Kamya Vrat - when Vrat is observed to fulfill any kind of desire.

In pushti sampradaya, it is not permitted to do Desire or Kamya Vrat because their devotees are completely dedicated to God and they believe that the Lord knows everything and he is omnipotent.

Age of Fasting

"अष्ट वर्शाधिको मर्त्यो अपूर्ण असिति वत्सर:

एकादश्यम उपावसेत पक्षयोर उभयोर अपि। "

One can start fasting after the age of 8 years and can continue till he is healthy.

(It is written in Hari-Bhakti Vilasa, Katyayan Smriti 12/75)

Who can observe vrat:

All menus and detailed information about Ekadashi are written in Hari-Bhakti Vilasa. The significance of Ekadashi is shown as a conversation between Lord Shiva and Devi Parvati in Padma Purana and the 12th chapter Hari-Bhakti Vilasa Brahma

Nardiya Puran and other religious texts mention the importance of Ekadashi Vrat as;

एकादशी व्रतम् नाम सर्व कामफलप्रदम

कर्तव्यम् सर्वदा विप्रै: विष्णु प्रिणनन कारणाम।

वर्णनम् आसरम् मनन्का स्रीना चा वर वर्णीनीम्

एकद्श्य् उपवासतु कर्तव्या ना अतरा स्मास्य:।

People of all Varna/castes that are Brahmin, Kshatriya, vaishya, shudra, and married, unmarried, widow, Male or female everyone can observe Ekadashi Vrat. We have to observe Ekadashi Vrat just not only to fulfill our desires but also to receive the grace of the Lord, to be closer to him, and for eternal peace and happiness.

उपवृतास्य पापेभ्यो अस्तुवासो गुणै: सह।

उपवास: स विज्ञेय: सर्व भोग विवीर्जीत:।।

On the auspicious day of Ekadashi, one has to try to be away from material happiness and activities restricted by religion like condemning someone. One should do devotional service and try to be near to the Lord.

(It is described in 13th and 14th verses of Hari bhakti Vilasa, parishishta katyayan Smriti, Vishnu Dharma and Brahma Vaiyatra Purana.)

पत्यौ जीवति या नार्युपोष्यव्रतमाचरेत्

आयुष्यं हरते भर्तु: सा नारी नरकं व्रजेत्।

It is written in Chapter 4 verses 17 of Parashar Smriti, chapter 12 15, and the 25th of Vishnu Smriti and shankh likhita Granth that Lord Vishnu describes that a married woman should never have to keep any fast without the permission of her husband. If married women disobey their husbands and observe fast then they will go to hell after their death and the lifespan of their husband also decreases.

*****

4. The benefits of the Ekadashi Vrat

Each Ekadashi has its significance and unique result that is described in every Ekadashi story. Ekadashi has great importance for Lord Vishnu and that is why it is said that people who observe Ekadashi Vrat will get moksha. (Free from the cycle of birth and death).

In ancient times there was a king named Mandhata. He was observing Ekadashi Vrat regularly, and due to the virtue of regular fasting on Ekadashi, he became a great emperor.

A long time ago there was a king called Rukmangada. He was a great devotee of Lord Vishnu and a very good and pious king. He was regularly fasting on Ekadashi day and at night he was reading holy books, doing prayers, and meditating for Lord Vishnu. Due to its virtue, he got Moksh after death.

Apart from that a person who observes the Ekadashi Vrat regularly, its fruits are equivalent to more than a hundred times doing Ashwamegh Yagya, ten times more than what he gets after donating thousands of cows, donating cows during a solar or lunar eclipse in Kurukshetra and providing food to needy during calamities like drought, etc.

(Summary from 125th chapter of Garuda Purana)

*****

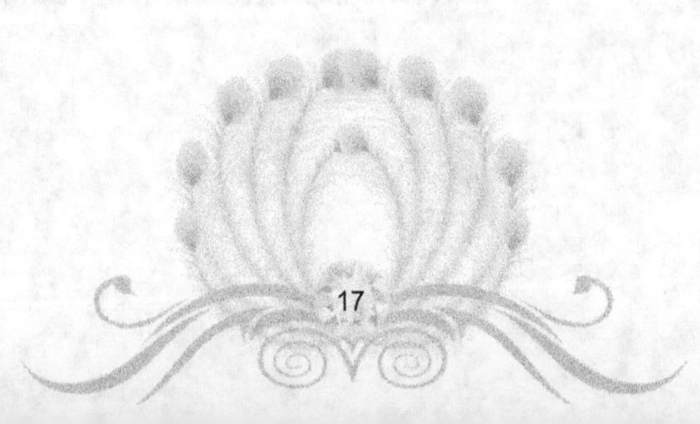

5. Food patterns of the Ekadashi day

As per the religious texts usually, one should not consume anything during the Ekadashi fast, that is neither food nor water. Those who find it difficult can consume only water. If it is not possible to fast only on the water then one can have milk and fruits and even if that is not possible then one can have fruits and beetroots, but one should abstain from grains and pulses. According to the Padma Purana, those who wish to attain 'Moksha' should not consume food made out of wheat, rice, pulses, bajra, and maida on the fast. It is also said that consuming grains and pulses while fasting is considered a sin. The story behind this is as per the order of Lord Vishnu, sin resides in grains and pulses on Ekadashi day. For making Ekadashi recipes spices like black salt, pepper, green chilies, dry ginger powder, and cumin can be used. Peanut or sesame oil, coconut, milk, and curd are also allowed for cooking. Apart from that potatoes, sweet potatoes, yam, purple yam, peanuts, and tapioca (sabudana) can also be used for cooking. Flours that are even consumed are Amarnath (rajgaro), kuttu, shingoda, and moraiyo which are considered as food of the saints and can be consumed after cooking and offering to the Lord.

One cannot eat regular food on that day.

(This verse about food patterns is written in Hari-Bhakti Vilasa sárga12-40.)

अष्टैतानियव्रतङ्गतानि आपेमूलंफलम पयः ।
हर्विब्राह्मण काम्याच गुरोवचनं मौषम् इति ।।

Means, water, fruits, milk, ghee, and beetroots are the five things that one can consume during the fast. One can consume all types of medicines also. One must follow the commands of their religious Gurus and participate in 'dana' (charity) to satisfy Brahmins. Ekadashi fast is completed post the sunrise of the following day.

*****

6. Ekadashi No Thal

Ho re,

Aaj Ekadashi chhe

Vishnu Bhagvan ne E vrat vahalu chhe, E vrat vahalu chhe ne

Moksha denarau chhe, tethi vaishnavo E vrat karyu chhe......

ho... ho... re

Koi kare Nirjala, ne koi kare faral, koi kare dudh pine

Koi kare ekvaar, mare to aaje najivu faral chhe......

ho...ho...re

Ekadashi chhe ne faral ni laher chhe......ho..ho..re

Barfi penda sathe dudhi no halvo chhe,

Kanda bateta ghee ma vagharel chhe

Farali chhevdo ne vefar no swad chhe......ho..ho..re

Shinghodana sheera sathe dudhi na muthiya chhe

Sabudana vada sathe bateta ni petis chhe

Taleli shing ma mari mitha no swad chhe......

ho...ho...re

Kesri Shrikhand sathe rajgara ni puri chhe

Suki Bhaji ma masalo bharpur chhe

Kuti dara na dhokda ma mari no swad chhe......

ho... ho...re

Sama ni khichdi sathe dahi ni kadhi chhe

Farfar papad sathe raitu taiyaar chhe

Khati mithi chatni ma tikho swad chhe......

ho...ho...re

Kesar masala nu kadhiyal dudh chhe

Yamuna jal ni zari bhari chhe

Mukhwas ma elaichi no sundar swad chhe......

ho...ho...re

****

7. Prasad on the day of Ekadashi

In Every temple, different food is offered to the Lord. Which is known as Prasad. The food which is offered to Lord Jagannath in the temple of Jagannath Puri is known as Mahaprasad.

There are different opinions about consuming prasad on Ekadashi day. According to the Hindu religion, prasad is very sacred and one can have it any day including Ekadashi even if it is made from grains and pulses. Whereas in Pushti sampradaya as per the command given by Shri Mahaprabhuji one cannot eat prasad on Ekadashi day which is made from grains and pulses, so pushti devotees consume prasad on the following day.

One incident of Shri Mahaprabhuji's life is given about this belief.

Once Mahaprabhuji reached Jagganaath Puri on Ekadashi day while traveling across India. One Brahmin of Godiya Sampraday gave Mahaprasad to him, but he was fasting. To maintain the respect of both the fast and Mahaprasad, Shri Mahaprabhuji kept it in his hand and consumed it the following day after the completion of his fast.

*****

8. Ekadashi Mata Ni Aarti

Jay Ekadashi MataJay Ekadashi Mata...ॐ

Moor daitya ne han-nari, devone tar-nari

Bhaktone bhakti aapti, kshn-ma sankat door karti

Jagat Janni, palanhari, gaurav aapti ... ॐ

24 roopwali, bare maas ma pujati tara naam ganavu

devi...ॐ

Kartak sud-ma Dev Uthi, vad-ma Utaptti kahevai;

Magsar sud-ma Mokshda, vad-ma Safala kahevai;

Posh sud-ma Putrada, vad-ma Shat-tila kahevai;

Maha sud-ma Jaya,vad-ma Vijya kahevai;

Fagan sud-ma Amalki, vad-ma Pap- mochini kahevai;

Chaitra sud-ma Kamda, vad-ma Varuthini kahevai;

Vaishakh sud-ma Mohini, vad-ma Apra kahevai;

Jeth sud-ma Nirjala, vad-ma Yogini kahevai;

Ashadh sud-ma Devshayani, vad-ma Kamika kahevai;

Shravan sud-ma Pavitra, vad-ma Aja kahevai;

Bhadarva sud-ma Parivartini, vad-ma Indira kahevai;

Aaso sud-ma Pashakunsha vad-ma Rama kahevai;

Purshottam sud-ma Padmini, vad-ma Parma kahevai;

Vishnu Pooja Vrat kari, Shakti Mukti pame;

Dard mate tan-nu, sukh sampati pame ॐ……

Ekadashi Mata -ni aarti je koi Jan gaaye;

Eno Vaikuntha ma vaas thay ॐ….

*****

9. Ekadashi Mahatmya Nu Bhajan

Aaj mare Ekadashi upvas, Mohan suno mara man ni vaat

Etle bolya sri Ghanshyam, Gopio sunjo kahu ek vaat

Jaine Gokul ma rahejo re, Ekadashi nu Mahatmya kahejo re

Avyo dasham tithi kero din, ekvaar jamvanu matam

Ekadashi na vanla vahay, datan kari ne sahu nahava jaay

Raate Jagran karva jaay, mukhe gun govind na gaaye

Ave baras tithi kero din, parna pahela karva punya

Mangavo adhik ujala anna, mare karva chhe maha punya

Taj, tel, Sopari ne vaitank, e tran chij no karvo tyag

Jivda jevi janeta taari, evi jaanje par ni nari

'Jiv' tane sachu kahu chhu saras, tujne taari deshe tarat

Mahatmya Ekadashi nu je gaaye, eno hojo vraj ma vaas.

******

10. The scientific significance of Ekadashi

71% of the Earth's surface is covered by water in the form of oceans, seas, and other water bodies. High and low tides in the oceans are caused by the moon's gravitational pull. This pull is higher during the seventh to the fifteenth days, In the lunar cycle of the lunar month.

The human body contains around 60%. water. Psychologists have concluded after scientific research that the moon's gravitational force not only affects the water bodies but also has an impact on the human mind, health, and behavior. People suffering from mental illness or mental stress feel more anxiety, depression, and insomnia between the seventh to fifteenth days, in both the lunar phases. During this period, it creates an imbalance between hormones, cells, and secretion from different glands.

1) Atmospheric pressure on the earth is highest on the 15th day of each lunar phase and it has a great impact on the physical and mental balance of human beings. Scientifically it takes 3 to 4 days for food to reach the brain. According to these calculations if we consume very less or no food on Ekadashi day it will help bridge the imbalance between the hormones.

2) If we fast on a day when atmospheric pressure is high then the mental and physical system of the body gets affected. In each lunar phase, atmospheric pressure is lowest on the eleventh day compared to other days and that is why 'Ekadashi' or the eleventh day of each lunar phase is considered a perfectly appropriate day for keeping fast.

One's intake of food and water is less on Ekadashi day due to fasting, which helps his inner gravitational force to become more powerful. As a result, it becomes easy for the body to balance with the moon's outer gravitational pull. This controls the functions of the organs like the liver, intestine, and kidneys, chemical changes, glands, cells, and other biological changes. Which also helps to control the negative effect on the body and mind.

*****

11. Pushti path - Pravah path and Maryada path

Pushti path, Maryada path, and Pravah path are all these three paths or ways in the spiritual journey that are different from each other and they all have their specialty.

PushtiMarg is a way of complete devotion towards the Supernatural and formless Lord.

The devotees who follow the path shown by religious texts of Hinduism and by maintaining its dignity try for their spiritual upliftment by any means of knowledge (Gyan), Karma, or devotion (bhakti) that path is known as the 'Maryada path.'

Those who get completely attached to the physical world and try to achieve only material happiness that path is known as 'Pravah Marg'.

Mahaprabhu Shri Vallabhacharya's principles are based on the four most important texts of Hinduism, namely:

- Vedas
- Brahmasutra
- Geeta
- Shrimad Bhagwat

All these four books are collectively known as 'Praman Chatushtaya.'

To give the complete knowledge of pushti sampradaya to his devotees Shri Mahaprabhuji has written different books at different times. Among them, the main sixteen books are known as 'Shodash Granth' or 'Shri Vallabh Geeta.'

They are as follows;

- Shri Yamunashtak
- Balbodh
- Siddhant muktavali
- Pushti Pravah Maryada bhed
- Siddhant Rahasya
- Navratna
- Antah Karan Prabodh
- Vivek Dhairyashray
- Krushnashray
- Chatu: shloki
- Bhakti vardhini
- Jala bhed
- Panch Padhyaani
- Sanyas Nirnay
- Nirodh lakshan
- Sevafal

Shrimad Bhagwat Geeta clearly describes that there are two types of human characters 'Daivi' and 'Asuri.' This principle is widely accepted even today. Shri Mahaprabhuji was also following Bhagavad Gita and that is why he was also believing in this principle. Over some time, with further studies he concluded that humans with Daivi characteristics are also divided into 'pushti Jiv (person, soul)' and 'Maryada Jiv' and they both are different. He made a detailed study of this and established it as a principle in his later age. He wrote the book 'Pushti -Pravah- Maryada bhed (difference)' during his constant stay in Adel.

There are some verses given below which helps to understand this concept more clearly.

पुष्टि-प्रवाह-मर्यादा विशेषण पृथक्-पृथक् ।
जीव-देह-क्रिया-भेदैः प्रवाहेण फलेन च ॥
वक्ष्यामि सर्वसन्देहा न भविष्यन्ति यच्छ्रुतेः ।
भक्तिमार्गस्य कथनात् पुष्टिरस्तीति निश्चयः ॥

Explanation.

Pushti, Pravah, and Maryada all these three paths are different from each other. I will explain the difference between their soul, body, working, thoughts, and fruition in detail, after listening that all doubts will be clear. The 12th chapter of Srimad Bhagavad Gita is all about 'Bhakti Marg' (path of devotion). It explains the characteristics of the Lord's true devotee (Bhakta). After listening it becomes clear that PushtiMarg is the path of the Lord's grace.

"द्वौ भूतसर्गा" इत्युक्तेः प्रवाहोऽपि व्यवस्थितः ।
वेदस्य विद्यमानत्वात् मर्यादापि व्यवस्थिता ॥

Explanation

The sixth verse in the 16th chapter of Srimad Bhagavad Gita starts with the word 'Dwavau bhutsargo' (two types of human characteristics) and further tells that these two types are 'Daivi 'and 'Asuri.' this verse of Gita proves that existence of 'Pravah-Marg ' is there. Apart from that, the existence of Vedas proves that Maryada Marg also exists.

कश्चिद् देवर्षि भक्तोऽहि यो मद्भक्त इतीरणात् ।
सर्वत्रोत्कर्षकथनात् पुष्टिरस्तीति निश्चयः ॥
न सर्वोऽतः प्रवाहाद्धि भिन्नो वेदाच्च भेदतः ।
'यदा येस्ये' ति वचनात् "नाहं वेदैः" इतीरणात् ॥

The 12th chapter of Srimad Bhagavad Gita describes the significance of his true devotees. While explaining the characteristics of his true devotee (Bhakta) many times Lord Krishna mentioned, 'I Love my true devotee. 'This explanation proves that there are only a few true devotees of the Lord and they are different from others.

In the fifty-third shloka of the 11th chapter, Lord says that one may study all Vedas, may do a lot of penance or may do a lot of charity yet he cannot see me. This explanation also proves that all humans (jiva) are not the same. They all are different from each other and the path they select for their spiritual journey is also different. From the above explanation, it is clear that PushtiMarg, Pravah-Marg, and Maryada Marg are different from each other. (4,5)

*****

12. 26 Ekadashi Stories

1) Prabodhini Ekadashi

<u>Prabodhini Ekadashi or Dev uthi Ekadashi: -</u> Kartak month Shukla paksha/ waxing phase.

The Shukla paksha Ekadashi of Kartak month is known as Prabodhini Ekadashi. As per the Hindu (Vikram samvat) calendar, this is the first Ekadashi of the year. Four months of monsoon are generally known as chaturmas. During this period Lord Vishnu rests in the milk ocean called Kshirsagar. On this Ekadashi day, he awakens. So, it is known as Dev uthi Ekadashi. It is also said that Lord Vishnu returned to his place from King Bali's court on this day. During these four months of the chaturmas, devotees observe some Vrats and worship the Lord. They feel the separation from their Lord because the Lord was resting. Due to the vrats and prayers of the devotees, the Lord awakens in their hearts also and their spiritual journey gets a boost. This is another reason that this Ekadashi is known as Dev uthi Ekadashi. The conversation between Lord Brahma and Narad Muni has described the significance of this Ekadashi.

Ekadashi story.

Once Narad Muni asked Lord Brahma, Oh father! Please explain to me about Prabodhini Ekadashi and its benefits.

Lord Brahma replied, my dear son, All Ekadashi has great importance for Lord Vishnu, so one has to observe this vrat for eternal happiness and prosperity.

There is a great virtue in doing Prabodhini Ekadashi, if you observe this Vrat you will be blessed with all your desires even if it is extremely difficult to achieve. You will be blessed with all kinds of physical and material happiness. bad deeds of previous birth will be destroyed. Those who observe this Vrat with full faith in it, their forefathers get placed in Vaikuntha Dham. Sins like Brahmahatya also destroy if one keeps awake and chants on Ekadashi night. There is a great virtue in performing yagna, donating, and chanting and it remains forever.

Lord Brahma continued; one has to decide about observing this Vrat in the very early morning in Brahma muhurta of Ekadashi day.

After that, he should have to worship the Lord with flowers, sandals, dhoop, deep, etc. Those who perform puja with flowers like rose, ashok, or bakul get freedom from the cycle of birth and death. Ekadashi night should be spent with holy activities like singing Bhajans and Kirtan, reading religious taxes, literature, etc. The Next day early morning, after bathing, one has to worship the Lord and perform the Puja for the Guru. Later he has to donate to the Brahmins and complete the vrat. Those who observe this vrat will be blessed with heaven and remain eternally happy,

One can restart consuming those things which he has given up during chaturmas.

As per the mythological story, a girl named Vrinda was born into a demon family but she was quite different. She was a great devotee of Lord Vishnu from her childhood and was always dedicated to his worship. When she grew up her parents arranged her marriage to a demon named Jalandhar. Jalandhar was born from 'Samundra-Manthan 'so he had great evil powers. Vrinda was a virtuous wife, apart from that whenever he went to battle, she was praying for him. Due to her selfless devotion, Jalandhar became more powerful and it was difficult to defeat or kill him. Once he started a battle with Devtas and defeated them all. Helpless Devtas went to Lord Vishnu and prayed for rescue. Lord Vishnu took the form of a Jalandhar demon. Vrinda was misguided and accepted him as a husband. As a misconception by Vrunda, Jalandhar's powers declined and got killed in the war. When Vrinda came to know about the truth that Lord Vishnu had cheated on her, she became very angry. She cursed him and made him a stone.

It was very shocking for everyone on earth to see Lord Vishnu in the form of a stone, which created chaos among the Devtas. Goddess Laxmi went to Vrinda and requested her to reverse the curse. Vrinda was a good-hearted and kind lady, for the welfare of the entire mankind she reversed the curse and became 'Sati' (Sacrificed herself) with her husband Jalandhar. A small tree grew from their destroyed bodies over some time. Lord Vishnu named that plant 'Tulsi,' and declared that I will not accept any of my offerings without Tulsi. This stone will be known as 'Shaligram' and has always been worshipped with Tulsi. Every year in Kartik month devotees celebrate the 'Tulsi Vivah' in which Tulsi and shaligram get married.

Views and Significance according to Pushti Sampraday:

The festival of prabodhini Ekadashi has a lot of importance in Pushti sampradaya. Every temple celebrates Tulsi Vivah on this day. In the story of Vrinda and the Jalandhar demon, Vrinda was a devotee of Lord Vishnu and a virtuous lady. So the Lord always remained in her heart. When she got enlightenment, she decided to marry Lord Vishnu. As a result, she was reborn as 'Tulsi' and the Lord became 'Shaligram' and they got married on prabodhini Ekadashi day.

There is another story of the era 'Saraswat Kalpa (eon or the period when Lord Vishnu has incarnated as Krishna). It is said that teenage Lord Krishna has enlightened Shri swaminiji, Radha, and the people of Gokul with all about his incarnation and all work he was going to do as a Krishna on the day of Prabodhini Ekadashi. He also made them experience happiness which occurs with the Lord's attachments.

Thus, Prabodhini Ekadashi also had significance in the Lord's secret activities.

Views and Significance according to ' Maryada-Marg':

According to the 'Skanda Purana,' Lord Vishnu took a rest for four months in the milk ocean (Kshirsagar) after killing the demon Shankhasur. 'He wakes up on the day of Prabodhini Ekadashi and that night got married to Tulsiji. Devotees of the Maryada path also celebrate Tulsi Vivah in the temples or at home.

Offering to Lord Vishnu

Kachoris (a snack made with green peas or green pigeon peas) is offered to God as a Prasad.

<u>**Benefits of observing Prabodhini Ekadashi vrat**</u>

The virtue of this fast is equivalent to performing one thousand Ashwamegh and Rajsuya Yagya each.

If one eats only one time in a day, get free from all sins of his lifespan.

If one eats only one time in the evening, get free from all sins of two lifespans.

And if one is completely fasting (without food) on this day, he will be free from all the sins of seven lifespans.

<u>**Small poem on prabodhini Ekadashi.**</u>

Raag - Kanharo

Dev jagavat Yashoda Maiya,

Fal fulan so puji kahat hai,

Chiranjivo mero kuvar kanhaiya ⎣ ⎣1⎣ ⎣

Tumhare jage kushal gokul ki,

badhe doodh aur Gaiya ⎣

' Govind' Prabhu Balaram Krishna ki,

lago mohi ballaiya ⎣ ⎣2⎣ ⎣

*****

2) Utapatti Ekadashi

<u>**Utapatti Ekadashi**</u> - Kartak Vad paksha /waning phase.

Lord Sri Krishna had told the importance of this Ekadashi to Arjun for the welfare of Mankind. He also said to Arjun that this Ekadashi is known as utpatti Ekadashi because mother Ekadashi was born on this day.

Ekadashi Story

Many years ago, there was a great, powerful and cruel demon named 'Taljangh', Who was believed to be a descendant of Lord Brahma? He had a son whose name was Moor, who was much more powerful and cruel than his father. He was staying in the famous city known as Chandrawati. Once he attacked devtas and defeated Indra, the king of Devtas, and declared himself a King. He expelled all devtas and Indra from heaven. The defeated devtas were roaming on earth in suspicion and fear.

They were very confused about what to do! Where to go? To find the solution they all went to Lord Shiva, Indra narrated the whole incident to him and added, "Moor has expelled us from our home and that is why we are roaming on earth, we are not comfortable with humans. You are our Lord, please help and guide us. How can we find a solution to this problem?" Lord Shiva advised them to go to Lord Vishnu and ask for help.

Indra became happy to hear this. Immediately he followed the advice and went to the milk ocean, known as Kshirsagar along with all the Devtas, where Lord Vishnu was resting. When they met Lord Vishnu, they prayed to him and requested him to save them from Moor's torture. Indra says, "Oh Lord, please accept our adoration. You are the creator and father of the whole world. You are the only reason behind each and everyone's existence. You are worshipped not only by devtas and humans but also by demons. We are very scared of Moor because he defeated us and expelled us from our homes, not only that he also captured our court along with his demon allies and dethroned us from our posts. we need your help. We know that you help your devotees fight against evils. Please save us."

Lord Vishnu gives them condolences and assures them that he will fight against Moor. Who was the king of Chandrawati and harassing people and Devtas over there? They were running in different directions due to his fear. Lord Vishnu went to Chandrawati along with devtas. When Moor saw them, he became very angry and called them for a fight. Lord Vishnu accepted the call and war started between them.

Lord Vishnu killed thousands of demon soldiers with his bow and arrow and Sudarshan chakra but Moor was still fighting. To misguide the Moor, the Lord went to a very long, (12 yojana) cave named Sinhawati in Badrikashram. It had only one gate. The Lord went deep inside and slept peacefully. Moor was following him when he reached there, he saw that Lord Vishnu was sleeping. He thought, he is the one from whom all demons are scared, it is better to kill him now only and if I do that we will be more powerful. When he was thinking this, suddenly a girl appeared from Lord's body. She was very beautiful, brave, and gorgeous. She was a great warrior and had many weapons in her hand. She looked like a powerful goddess.

When Moor looked at that divine girl, she asked him to do war with her. Moor accepted the challenge and war began between them.   The divine girl was excellent in all types of war techniques, very soon she defeated Moor and killed him. After some time when Lord Vishnu woke up, he saw that Moor had been killed and one divine girl was standing nearby.   He was surprised and asked, who killed this powerful and cruel demon? The divine girl replied, I am goddess Ekadashi and I killed him. Lord Vishnu was pleased with her answer and blessed her.

Views and significance according to Pushti Sampraday

Females of Gokul (vrajkumarika) observe a Katyayani Vrat for receiving Krishna as their husband. On this Ekadashi day, they created the first sculpture of Katyayani Devi from the sand (renu) of Sri Yamuna River, that is why this Ekadashi is known as 'Utpatti Ekadashi'. It has great importance in Pushti sampradaya.

Aspects of Maryada Path

The aspect of Maryada Marg follows the same story of the Moor demon. Goddess Ekadashi was born from the body of Lord Vishnu to kill the demon Moor on this day and that is why this Ekadashi is known as Utapatti Ekadashi.

Offerings to Lord Vishnu

Almonds are to be offered to Lord Vishnu on this day.

Benefits

Previous birth's sins are destroyed.

According to the 'Bhavishyottara Purana,' the benefit is as equivalent to donating a thousand cows.

As per religious text, the one who observes this Vrat will attain Vaikuntha Dham.

Only knowing and listening about this Ekadashi also has a great effect. It gives freedom from sins like Brahma hatya.

Aarti

Jay Utapatti ekadashi,

Jay Utapatti ekadashi

Hemant rutuma aj tu pragat thaye

Kartak mahine tari Puja gaaye

Krishna paksha ni ghadi maj tu j param Data......Jay ...Jay

Shatruono naash tu karti,

tu Jivma moksha bharti

Tari bhakti karvathi ashwamegh na fal malta......Jay ...Jay

Te Arjun-ne fal didhu,

tenu te kam kidhu,

Stuti karayathi sau kamo ahi falta .....Jay.....Jay

Vishnu lokma vaas taro,

Udhhar kar je tu maro,

Tu param krupalu tu j che data..............Jay ...Jay

Utapatti ekadashi.

*****

3) Mokshda Ekadashi

<u>Mokshda Ekadashi</u> - Magsar Sud-Shukla paksha/waxing phase.

Lord Sri Krishna has explained the significance of Mokshda Ekadashi to king Yudhishthira. There is a great virtue in keeping this Ekadashi Vrat.

<u>Story</u>

Once upon a time, there was a king named 'Vaikhanas'. His Kingdom was very beautiful, known as Champak / Kampka / Gokul Nagar.

King Vaikhanas was brave, adventurous, and good-hearted and took very good care of his subjects. People were very happy in his kingdom. One day he had a dream and he saw that all his forefathers were suffering in hell. They all were very sad and unhappy and repeatedly pleaded to save their souls. The King became very upset after this dream. He thought that he should do something for his forefathers, but he was not aware of what he could do! The next morning, he narrated this incident to all Brahmins in his court and asked, "Please show me some way, Vrat or penance, by practicing that I can save my ancestors. My life has no meaning if I can't do anything for them." All Brahmins replied to him," your majesty, you should take advice from 'Maharshi Parbat'. He is very knowledgeable and aware of the past, present, and future. His ashram is also nearby.

King immediately followed the advice and went to the ashram of 'Maharishi Parbat'.

King bowed down to the rishi and touched his feet. Rishi Parbat welcomed him and asked, "if there was political stability and prosperity in his Kingdom?" The King replied," Munivar, all is well with your grace but a few days ago I had a dream and I saw that all my ancestors are suffering in hell. I wish to free them. Can you please suggest any solution? After listening to this the sage sat in meditation for about one and half hours (one muhurta time). After waking up from meditation he replied, "O great king! You observe the vrat of magsar shukla Ekadashi and pass on that virtue to your forefathers. Due to the influence of that virtue, they will be free from hell and their suffering."

King returned from the ashram happily. After some time when magsar month came he observed the Ekadashi Vrat and passed on that virtue to his ancestors as per the Rishi's advice. Due to that, king Vaikhanas's ancestors were freed from hell. They became very happy and appeared in the sky to bless him. They showered him with flowers and said, 'Dear son you and your kingdom will always prosper'. After that, they disappeared and went to heaven.

Thus, those who keep this Vrat will be free from all sins, their all desires will be fulfilled and they attain Moksha after death. This Ekadashi is known as Mokshada Ekadashi because it gives Moksha or Heaven to a 'Jivatma.'

As per Brahmanda Purana, those who keep this Vrat and worship Lord with Puja Aarti and bhajan he will get the virtue of 'Vajpeya Yagya', apart from that any of his family members or near ones whose souls suffer in hell or are damned souls are freed and placed in heaven.

Views and significance according to Pushti Sampraday

As per the reference to the context of PushtiMarg Lord Sri Krishna kills the demon 'Putna' and provides her Moksha on this auspicious day of magsar shukla Ekadashi and that is why this Ekadashi is known as mokshada Ekadashi.

Views according to Maryada Path.

The war between Kauravas and Pandavas on the battlefield of Kurukshetra started on this day. Sri Krishna preached 'Shrimad Bhagavad Gita' to Arjun also on this day therefore this day is also known as 'Gita Jayanti'. It is said that the person who recites or listens to all slokas of Shrimad Bhagavad Gita will surely attain moksha and that is why also this Ekadashi is known as mokshada Ekadashi.

Offering to Lord Vishnu

Recipes made from Amaranth flour are generally offered to Lord Vishnu on this day / Rajgira Shira.

Benefits

One who observes this Vrat will be freed from all sins and will benefit from the virtue of 'Vaishya Tapasya's.

Aarti of Mokhsda Ekadashi

Jay Jay Mokshda Ekadashi.

Jay Mokshda Ekadashi

Magsar maas ma malti Shukla paksha ma falti

Vaikhasan e parivaar,

Brahman,

prajajan sahit kari bhakti

Mukti apavi paap thi,

Pitane Udhharya ......

Jay Jay

Mokshda Ekadashi.

*****

4) Safala Ekadashi

<u>**Safala Ekadashi**</u> - Magsar Vad paksh/ waning phase.

Lord Sri Krishna has explained the significance of Safala Ekadashi to king Yudhisthira. He told him that those who keep this Vrat will attain all kinds of happiness and all his sins will be destroyed.

Story

Long ago there was a king named Mahishman. His kingdom Champawati was very famous and beautiful. The King had four sons among them his eldest son was always engaged in sinful deeds. Instead of taking interest in studies and taking care of his Kingdom, he used to spend his father's wealth on activities like gambling and prostitution. He was immoral and an atheist, he also disrespected and humored God, Brahmins, and

Vaishnavas. Due to such behavior, his father named him 'Lumpak' and expelled him from his kingdom. His brothers supported their father in punishing 'Lumpak'.

Lumpak started living deep inside the forest on one very old peepal tree. For satisfying hunger, he ate fruits and meat, and to cope with his financial needs he became a thief in his father's kingdom, not only that he also started hitting and torturing the citizens. They were fed up with Lumpak's behavior but they were helpless. Sometimes the night guards caught him but since he was the king's son, they could not muster the courage to punish him.

One day due to physical weakness, tiredness, and ill health he didn't kill any animals for food nor was he able to stand up. At night he shivered in the cold due to a lack of clothes. He starved the whole day, and as a result, he became unconscious. This was the previous day of Ekadashi, i.e., Dasham tithi of magsar month's waning phase. When he got a sense, it was the afternoon of Ekadashi day. After some time, he collected some fruits and offered them to the peepal tree and said, O Lord Vishnu, please accept these fruits and be satisfied. (There is a belief that Lord Vishnu resides in a peepal tree) Thus, unknowingly he observes the Safala Ekadashi Vrat and because of this all his sins are destroyed and Lord Vishnu is pleased with him. The next morning one divine and beautifully decorated chariot suddenly appeared in front of him and he heard an oracle, "Lumpak all your sins are destroyed due to the influence of Lord Vishnu, now you should restart your life, you go to your father and rule your kingdom." Lumpak became happy after listening to these blessings. He went to his father, apologized, and narrated the incidents to him. He gave up all bad habits and became a devotee of Lord Vishnu. He started living decently with all responsibilities and he gained a divine glow.

King Mahishman saw the changed behavior of his son and was so pleased that he abdicated the throne in the name of his son and went to the forest to live as Sanyasi. After that Lumpak ruled his kingdom Champawati very well and as per the norms of religious texts for about fifteen years. His wife and son were also great devotees of Lord Vishnu. He named his son Manogya. When Lumpak became old he gave his throne to Manogya and went into the forest just like his father to worship Lord. He attained Moksha after death.

Views and significance as per pushtimarg

All gopis of Vraj (Gokul and surrounding area) had true devotion towards Shri Krishna. The aim of their devotional services was only to create closeness with the Lord. They never desire any material happiness but wish to get Lord Krishna as their husband. They observed Katyayani Vrat for that reason and their wish gets fulfilled on this day and that is why this Ekadashi is known as Safala Ekadashi.

Views according to Maryada Path.

Arjun won the battle of Mahabharata with the grace and support of Lord Shri Krishna.

On this day after the war, Arjun rested under the peepal tree and enjoyed his victory. That is why this Ekadashi is known as Safala Ekadashi.

Offering to Lord Vishnu

Sesame seeds are supposed to be offered to Lord Vishnu on this day.

<u>**Benefits**</u>

Anyone who performs this Vrat attains virtues similar to those received while performing the Ashwamegh Yagya. Moreover, they also gain name and fame in this life and attain Moksha after death.

<u>**Aarti**</u>

Jay Jay Safala mata,

Jay Jay Safala mata

Magsar maas ma malti,

Krishna Paksha ma falti.... Ma... (2)

Safal Jeevan karnari,

tu chhe param data......

Jay Jay Safala mata

Lumpak ne tame taaryo,

eno aham maaryo ....ma.... (2)

Param pad denari,

tu evi mata ......

Jay Jay Safala mata

Sarve dukho ne taadya,

sarve papone te baadya ....ma... (2)

Ati sukhdayi,

tuj geet gata............

Jay Jay Safala mata

Karma tare angne fadta,

dharma tare angne madta....ma... (2)

Darek rahasya khuulu,

he devi tame karta...

Jay Jay Safala mata

*****

5) Putrada Ekadashi

<u>Putrada Ekadashi</u> - Posh month waxing phase Ekadashi/ Shukla Ekadashi.

According to the Hindu calendar, the eleventh tithi of Posh month's waxing phase is known as Putrada Ekadashi. The significance and story of this Ekadashi are described by Lord Sri Krishna to the king Yudhisthira.

<u>Story</u>

Long ago a king named 'Suketuman' ruled the kingdom Of Bhadrawatipuri.

He was good-hearted and his administration was excellent therefore his subjects were happy. His wife, Queen Champa was also a virtuous lady. The King and queen were happy by all means but they had no heir who could carry forward their legacy and that is why they were unhappy. For many years they tried various medicines, herbs, yagna, etc. but to no avail. Even King Suketuman's forefathers, who were resting in heaven were worried about the continuation of their legacy?

Once, the king decided to go to the forest for mental peace and relaxation so he picked up his horse and rode there, his ministers were not aware of this. The forest was full of animals and birds like deer, bears, foxes, and owls. Admiring the natural beauty, he forgot the time and went deep inside the forest. When he felt hungry and thirsty, he realized that it was late noon. He saw a lake nearby and went towards it. When he reached the lake, he was surprised to see that many ashrams and sages were chanting Vedas on its bank. He became very happy to see them, he also experienced auspicious signs like the blinking of his right eye and right hand. He tied his horse to a tree and went near the sages and worshipped them. He gave his introduction to the Rishis and asked gently "Can you please tell me who you are? And what is the reason behind this collective chanting?" The sages replied, "King Suketuman! We are 'Vishwadeva'. Today's day is known as 'Putrada Ekadashi'. If one observes this Vrat he will be blessed with a son. We are here for a holy bath on this auspicious day. We are happy with your modesty; tell us what blessings you want?" King said, "I have no heir, if you are really happy, please bless me with a son." Sages blessed him and explained that you observe today's Ekadashi vrat. Lord Krishna will bless you with a baby boy.

King Suketuman stayed there and observed Putrada Ekadashi Vrat with devotion and as explained by sages. The next day he returned home with the blessing of sages after completing the Vrat. A few days later the queen conceived and gave birth to a beautiful baby boy. The prince was a well-mannered and bright child. The king and queen were happy with him. When he became young King Suketuman renounced his throne to his son. He became a wise and noble king who took great care of his subjects.

View and significance according to Pushti Sampraday

Ashta Sakha Kumbhandas and his wife seek blessings for having a son from Shri Mahaprabhuji on Putrada Ekadashi day. With the blessings of Mahaprabhuji Kumbhandas became the father of seven brilliant sons. They all were great devotees of Lord Sri Krishna. This Ekadashi is associated with the one incident of Lord Shrinathji's beloved Ashta Sakha Kumbhandas's life and that is why it has great importance in Pushti sampradaya.

Views as per Maryada Path.

In the Sanskrit language (other languages like Hindi and Gujarati also) son is called' Putra '. It is said that ' Putra ' saves from a hell called 'Pum'. As per this belief, those who observe this vrat will surely be blessed with a male child and attain heaven after death. This Ekadasi provides the happiness of a child and that is why it is known as Putrada Ekadashi.

Offerings to Lord Vishnu

Buttermilk and jaggery are supposed to be offered to Lord Vishnu on this day.

Benefits

Those who observe this Vrat will be blessed with a baby boy and also attain heaven after death. Those who listen to the significance of this Ekadashi will get the virtue of Ashwamegh Yagya.

Jay Jay Putrada mata,

Jay Jay Putrada mata

Posh mata malti,

Shukla paksha ma fadti......Ma... (2)

Prabhu narayan ni puja,

sarva dukho harati ......

Jay Jay Putrada mata

Putra ne prapta karavnari,

punya ne tu pragtavnari.... Ma ... (2)

Suketuman -ne putra,

dan evu karti..........

Jay Jay Putrada mata

Je koi sune Mahima katha,

eni jay sau vyatha....... Ma (2)

Rajane kidha kritagya,

evi taari gaatha.........

Jay Jay Putrada mata

***

6) Shat-Tila Ekadashi

Shat-Tila Ekadashi- Posh month's waning phase / Krishna Paksha.

Lord Sri Krishna has described the significance of Shat-Tila Ekadashi to Narad Muni. He said that Posh month's waning phase / Krishna Paksha Ekadashi is known as Shat-Tila Ekadashi. Rishi Gabhasti has also described the significance of this Ekadashi to Rishi Dalabhya.

Story

The story of this Ekadasi is also found in Purana; it relates to the pious Brahmin woman.

A long time ago there was a pious Brahmin woman. She was a great devotee of God. Her nature was good, she also observed various Vrats but she never donated any food or money to needy people or Brahmins. There is a lot of significance of charity during one's lifespan for the upliftment of the soul after death. Lord Vishnu got worried about this pious lady, he thought that this lady is very good but only because of her misery she would not be able to attain all the happiness in Vaikuntha Dham. I should help her because she is my true devotee. Lord Vishnu disguised himself as a Brahmin beggar and went to her home for bhiksha. The Brahmin lady gave him a lump of clay instead of food. Lord Vishnu took it and returned to Vaikuntha. Over some time after death, that lady went to the abode of God. There she got one empty hut and one mango tree. She was surprised to see that her house was empty. She went to Lord Vishnu and asked, I am very religious and your true devotee also. Yet, I have received an empty hut! What is the reason behind that? Lord Vishnu replied, it is true that you are very religious but till now you have neither done any kind of charity nor helped any needy people by providing food. When I came to your house and asked for bhiksha you gave me a lump of clay instead of food. That is why your hut is empty. The Brahmin lady realized her mistake. She asked, what should I do now to be free from this? Lord said wives of all Devtas will come to meet you. First, you ask them for all details and methods of doing Shat-Tila Ekadashi Vrat, after that open your hut for them. As per Lord Vishnu's advice, the Brahmin lady collected all details from the goddess and observed Shat-Tila Ekadashi Vrat with true devotion. As a result, she became beautiful and her hut got filled with grains, wealth, and gold.

PushtiMarg devotees every day worship Lord Krishna for all Krishna Leela's which Lord Shri Krishna performed in Vraj, Gokul when he was a child.

Devotee's feeling and emotions towards Leelas of Krishna during his childhood in Vraj is the predominant factor in Pushti Seva. Shri Mahaprabhuji and Shri Gusaiji have gracefully blended the concept of daily worship (Nitya Seva) whether at home or temple of Lord Krishna with his childhood Leelas like Govardhan puja, Rasleela, grazing cow herd, etc. Lord's robes, ornaments, and other offerings are also according to these Leelas.

(They've also considered religious taxes and nakshatra following that.)

On Shat-Tila day pushtimarg devotees offer sesame seed to Lord Krishna in six different ways like making him bathe with sesame seed, massaging him with sesame seed, offering khichdi or laddu made from sesame seed, etc.

Worship as per Maryada path

There is a lot of importance in the use of sesame seeds on this Ekadashi day. People usually use Sesame seeds in six different ways, such:

- For making various recipes
- As a sesame oil in food
- For medicines
- For body massage
- In yagya as offering (aahuti)
- To donate to someone

As per the significance described by Lord Sri Krishna to Narad Muni those who perform yagna with sesame seeds and donates sesame seed on this day will get rid of all sins.

Offerings to Lord Vishnu

Recipes made out of coconut and sesame seeds are supposed to be offered to Lord Vishnu on this day.

Benefits of this Ekadashi

If one observes this Ekadashi Vrat then his poverty and misfortune will perish and he will be wealthy. Those who donate sesame seeds on this day will get rid of all their sins.

Aarti

Jay Jay Shat-tila Ekadashi,

Jay Shat-tila Ekadashi

Posh maas na Krishna paksha ma aavti tal angikari

Pulatsya muni kahe tal daan,

lep, seven karta

Mukti apavi paapthi,

Narkagar thi bachave......

Jay Jay Shattilla Ekadashi.

*****

7) Jaya Ekadashi

<u>Jaya Ekadashi Maha Sud-</u> Shukla paksha/ waxing phase Ekadashi.

The importance of this Ekadashi is explained by Lord Sri Krishna to Narad Muni.

Lord Krishna explained the importance of Jaya Ekadashi to Narad Muni and said, "The eleventh tithi of 'Maha month 'in waxing phase is known as Jaya Ekadashi, and those who observe this Ekadashi Vrat, their all sin gets destroyed."

<u>Story of Ekadashi</u>

This story relates to King Indra, nymph (Apsara) Pushpavati, and Pushpadant Gandharva, who was also known as Malyavan.

Once king Indra arranged a music celebration in his court. All Devtas, Gandharvas, and Apsaras were present to enjoy music and dance (nritya). A Gandharva named Chitrasen was present with his wife Malini and his beautiful daughter pushpavati.

Another young Gandharva named Malyavan was also there. Pushpavati and Malyavan were performing together in the dance ceremony. While dancing they felt an attraction toward each other and fell in love because of which they were unable to coordinate with other dancers, and could not also concentrate on the music that was being played. Indira felt insulted and got angry. He cursed them and said, "Pushpavati and Malyavan you both are not attentive and creating a mess, you have also disobeyed my orders so I curse you that you both will be born as a vampire couple (as pitch demon) on earth. "They both became sad after getting cursed by Indra but they were helpless.

Soon they both turned into a vampire couple and reached earth. Suffering from the pain caused by physical agony both were wandering in the ravines of the Himalayas.

They were worried about how to get rid of the curse and horrible vampire form. Their health also deteriorated due to the anxiety and stress of the vampire form.

One day they were very sad. That was an auspicious day of 'Jaya Ekadashi'. They both fasted on that day. They didn't kill any animals for food, didn't have water, and didn't even cut or consume fruits. At night they were unable to sleep due to grief. The whole night they sat under a banyan tree. Both Vampires observed 'Jaya Ekadashi Vrat' who stayed up all night and due to the influence of that and Lord Vishnu's grace, they both were freed from the curse and got their original form of Gandharva back. They were adorned with beautiful garments and ornaments. Their hearts were filled with love towards each other. They both went to heaven in a plane and sought the blessings of King Indra.

Views and Significance as per Pushti Marg

When Shri Gusaiji was doing 'Vraj parikrama' (pilgrimage in the Vraj region) he came into contact with many such bogey souls (jivatma in bhoot - Pret yoni) who were suffering and wanted to be free. Shri Gusaiji saved and freed them. Apart from that, he helped many other ignoble people for their spiritual, religious, and physical upliftment. A Vaishnav named 'KrishnaDas Adhikari' had hostility towards Shri Gusaiji. He made him remove from Lord Srinathji's temple Seva but Shri Gusaiji got back that Seva and yet he didn't hold any grudge against KrishnaDas Adhikari, not only that he also helped him to get out when he fell in the well. He was very kind and generous and that is why he is also known as 'Shri Gusaiji Param Dayal'.

View as per Maryada Path

Two agents of Lord Vishnu named Jay and Vijay got cursed by a sage and were born as vampires (in pishach yoni). They were facing much physical pain and mental torture as Vampires. Once they didn't find any food, fruits, or water and remained hungry and thirsty for the whole day and night. That was the auspicious eleventh tithi i.e., Ekadashi of the waxing phase of Maha month. Unknowingly they both observe Ekadashi fast and due to that they both get rid of vampire form (pishach yoni) and receive blessings from Lord Vishnu. In the name of Jay and Vijaya, this Ekadashi is known as a Jaya Ekadashi.

Offerings to Lord Vishnu

Sugarcane is supposed to be offered to Lord Vishnu on this day.

<u>**Benefits of Ekadashi Vrat**</u>

If one observes this Vrat he will get rid of sins like brahmahatya and attain Vaikuntha Dham. If one listens or reads about this Ekadashi it will be considered equivalent to performing Agnistom yagna.

<u>**Aarti**</u>

Jay Jay Jaya Ekadashi,

Jay Jay Jaya Ekadashi,

Maha maase tu malti,

sarva jano- ne falti

Bhoot Pret bhage re,

bhay darne harti.........

Jay Jay Jaya Ekadashi,

Malyavan na ne taaryo,

bhoot pishach ne maryo,

Mukti apavi paapthi,

dushtane Uddharyo.........

Jay Jay Jaya Ekadashi,

Kuyonithi tu bachave,

Punya fal tu lave

Dan adine Karta,

Krupa Kari bachave......

Jay Jay Jaya Ekadashi,

*****

8) Vijaya Ekadashi

<u>Vijaya Ekadashi</u> - Maha Vad (Krishna paksha)/ waning phase.

The significance of Vijaya Ekadashi is explained by Lord Sri Krishna to king Yudhishthir. He said the eleventh tithi of the waning phase of Maha month is known as Vijaya Ekadashi.

<u>Ekadashi story</u>

Lord Brahma told Narad Muni that Vijaya Ekadashi Vrat has existed since ancient times and is very sacred. Any person, including the king, observing this Vrat will achieve victory.

The story of Vijaya Ekadashi is associated with Lord Vishnu's incarnation as Shri Ram in Treta Yuga. As per the story, when Shri Rama reached the ocean with Sugriva and his Vanar Sena he was confused about crossing the vast ocean! He asked his younger brother Lakshman, "what should we do to cross this ocean which is very deep, vast, and full of aquatic animals?

Lakshman replied, "Ashram of the great sage Shri Bakdabhalya Muni is around half yojana (Approximately 4 miles) far from here. I think we have to go there and seek his advice." Shri Rama agreed to that and they all went to the Ashram of Shri Bakdabhalya Muni and bowed down to him.   The sage welcomed them and asked how he could help them. Shri Rama asked, "Munivar! I want to fight against King Ravana and for that, I need to cross this vast ocean with my soldiers (Vanar Sena). So please suggest to me, how can I do that?"

The sage suggested, "Rama!   There is the Vrat of Vijaya Ekadashi which is on the eleventh tithi of the waning phase in Maha month. If you will keep this Vrat you will Surely be able to cross the ocean and get the victory."

Lord Brahma told Narad Muni, that as per the advice of sage Shri Bakdabhalya Muni Shri Rama observes this, Vrat. As a result, he conquered 'Lanka' (kingdom of Ravana)and killed King Ravana. Devi Sita was freed from King Ravana's custody in Ashok Vatika and Returned to Shri Ram.

Significance and views as per pushti Sampraday

Shri Mahaprabhuji had said, जीवाः स्वभावतः दुष्टाः It means or as per Shri Mahaprabhuji's perception every soul i.e 'Jiv' has qualities of God (Bramh) because they are separated from God. Due to the separation of God and connection with other virtues and sins on earth for a very long period every soul i.e. jiv gets affected by six types of flaws anger, greed, arrogance, jealousy, infatuation, and desire. To free them from these flaws Shri Mahaprabhuji suggested to devotees that their minds should remain attached to Lord Sri Krishna during seva and while performing other duties also. For remaining eternally attached to God he gave 'Brahma Sambandh' to his devotees, 'Brahma' means God and 'sambandh' means relation /attachment. He also gave Mantra, 'Shri Krishna Seva Sadakarya' means that devotees are supposed to stay engaged with Seva /worship of Lord Krishna. Few true devotees freed themselves or made victory from these six flaws like anger, greed, etc. with their devotional Seva on this auspicious day of Ekadashi and that is why this Ekadashi is known as Vijaya Ekadashi.

View as per Maryada Path.

According to the Skanda Purana Lord, Shri Ram started his journey to Lanka, after constructing a bridge on the ocean on the day of Vijaya Ekadashi. The journey for the victory of good and evil started on this auspicious day and that is why this day has a lot of importance. Those who observe this Ekadashi Vrat will surely achieve great success in all his works.

Offerings to Lord Vishnu: Penda

Benefits

One gets rid of all his sins and observes this, Vrat. Those who read or listen to this Ekadashi story will get the virtue of performing Vajpeya yagna.

Aarti

Jay Vijya Ekadashi,

Jay Jay Vijya Ekadashi,

Maha maase padhare,

Krishna Paksha ma vistare

Vijay sarve apave,

karma kare je dhaare..............

Jay Jay

Ram gaya par samudre,

madad kari e shundre

Kalash nichhe saat anaj,

je aa dine muke..........

Jay Jay

Swarna Pratima Narayan,

kare manma jo dharan

Vrat kare e manthi,

paaye swarg nu taran.............

Jay Jay

*****

9) Amalaki Ekadashi

Amalaki or Kunja Ekadashi- Fagan month Shukla paksha / waxing phase.

Ekadashi story

King Mandhata asked Rishi Vashishth about the waxing phase Ekadashi of Fagan month. As an answer, the Rishi explained that at the time of the cataclysm (pralaya) the world had been destroyed and turned into an ocean. After that, over some time one drop of Lord Vishnu's spit which was as glorious as the moon fell on earth. Eventually, an Amla (Amalaki) tree grew from that drop and over some time it became a giant tree. This tree is considered the 'Adi vrukha' (father of all trees). Parallel to this period, Lord Vishnu formed Lord Brahma for creating the universe. Lord Brahma created the universe and various species. He also created Devtas, demons, Gandharva, Yaksha, Raksha, Naag, and kind-hearted Maharishis.

Among them, Devtas and Maharishes reached the place where the Amla tree had grown. They had never seen this kind of tree and its fruits ever before. so, they were surprised and began to speculate about it. Suddenly there was an oracle, "Maharishi! This is the best and most revered tree of Amla. Lord Vishnu loves this tree and its fruit Amla. All Gods and Devtas reside in this tree, it is said that Lord Vishnu stays in the roots, Lord Brahma stays in the lower bark and Lord Shiva stays in its upper bark. Sages and Devtas live in its branchhes. The 'Vashu spices' live in its leaves, 'Marudgan' in flowers, and all other species live in its fruit Amla. It's a Vaishnav tree that destroys all your sins and that is why it is a pious tree for Vishnu devotees. One should consume Amla very happily. If one chants the name of this holy tree, he will get the virtue of donating cows. If one touches the tree, he will get two times and if one eats the fruit, he will get three times the virtue of donating cows."

After listening to this oracle, Maharishi asked, "please tell us who you are? Please give us your true introduction." The divine voice replied, "I am creator and operator of this universe, it's difficult to see me also for great virtuous people, I am Lord Vishnu."

Second story

In the olden days, king Chitrarath was ruling the kingdom Vidisha. Chitrarath's forefather king 'Pasbinduk' belonged to the Chandravanshi dynasty. King Chitrarath was not only truthful, kind, and generous but also a great devotee of Lord Vishnu. He was taking good care of his subjects and his subjects were also happy and full of devotion toward Lord Vishnu. They all observed Ekadashi fast regularly. There was a beautiful Vishnu temple and Amla (Amalaki) tree on the bank of the river in their kingdom. Once early in the morning on the day of Amalaki Ekadashi, the king and his subjects took a holy bath in the river and worshiped Lord Vishnu and the Amalaki tree. For the whole day and night, they were praying to the Lord with chanting and bhajans.

One dacait who was feeding himself by killing people came there on that night. Even though he was very hungry and thirsty he remained seated for the whole night and chanted holy names along with the king and his subjects. As a result of an unintentional devotional act done by him on Amalaki Ekadashi day, he got the next birth in the royal family. He was born Vasurath, son of the king Vidurath in the Jayanti kingdom. He was wise and brave like Lord Vishnu, bright like the sun, and a noble king and became an excellent ruler.

Views and significance as per Pushti Sampraday.

Amalki Ekadashi is also known as Kunj Ekadashi in Pushti Sampraday. From this day all Pushti temples started celebrating the Holi festival and continued till 'Dhuleti' or 'Doll Utsav' day. (Doll Utsav generally happens on the day of Uttara phalguni nakshatra) Once due to some problems in Mathura, Shri Giridharji celebrated all 'Darshans of Holi festival' (in temple Seva some festivals are celebrated outside the temple) inside the temple. Vaishnava devotees prepare a beautiful swing with flowers and mango leaves and decorate it with backdrops and hangings. Then they made the Lord sit in a swing and began with the 'Doll Utsav' celebration with abil, gulal, and wet color made from 'Kesuda' flowers. They repeat this darshan four times out of which three times they offer food, known as 'Bhog' to Lord. In those four darshans, three darshans have emotions of Krishna playing Holi with friends (Gop - Gopi of vraj) and the fourth darshan has intense emotions that one can understand easily once he develops himself spiritually.

<u>**Views as per Maryada path.**</u>

As per the story of Brahmanda Purana king, Chaitrarath observes this Ekadashi Vrat. King took a holy bath and put a pitcher pot (Kumbh) under the Amalaki tree. After that, he chanted for the whole day and night. Once the king's enemy attacked him when he was sleeping. Due to the accumulated virtues of Amalaki Ekadashi Vrat, one divine force appeared from the king's body and defeated his enemies.

<u>**Offerings to Lord Vishnu**</u>

Amla fruits are supposed to be offered to Lord Vishnu on this Ekadashi day.

<u>**Benefits**</u>

One who observes this Ekadashi Vrat will attain Vaikuntha Dham after death.

<u>**Aarti**</u>

Jay Jay Amalki Ekadashi,

Jay Amalki Ekadashi

Phalgun (Fagan) maas na Shukla paksha ma aavti,

Amalki angikari

Vishnu ne priya chhe,

sarva dev- may chhe,

Amalki vaishnava vruksh chhe

Vishnu Bhakta purusho mate param pujya chhe,

Amalki angikari

..........Jay Jay Amalki Ekadashi

*****

10) Papmochini Ekadashi

Papmochini Ekadashi- Fagan month Vad-Krishna Paksha / waning phase.

Lord Shri Krishna has described the significance of papmochini Ekadashi to king Yudhister. He said, "The eleventh tithi of waning phase in Fagan a month is known as papmochini Ekadashi.

Ekadashi story

A long time ago there was a brave king named Mandhata. Once King Mandhata asked Rishi Lomesh, how can one get free from all the sins which he has done knowingly or unknowingly? As an answer, Rishi told a story to him. Long ago there was a forest known as Chitrarath. The forest was very beautiful and full of fragrant flowers. Indra Dev and other Devtas, Apsaras, and daughters of the Gandharvas with their musical instruments were frequently visiting this forest for their recreation. They roamed or enjoyed music in a pleasant atmosphere. In this forest, there was an ashram of Rishi Medhavi. He was a great sage, for many years he was doing 'Tapasya' and living with chastity and celibacy (brahmacharya). Many Apsaras try to break his 'Tapasya' (Penance) but they did not succeed. An Apsara named Manjughosha decided to break the Tapasya of Rishi Medhavi and came to the forest to attract him. She was aware that if she directly went in front of him, he might curse her so she stopped at a distance from the ashram and started singing beautiful songs and playing Veena. When Rishi Medhavi reached there while roaming, he listened to the beautiful voice and soothing music of Manjughosha. He went further to see who was singing and playing the music! When he saw Manjughosha, he got attracted by her beauty and her melodious voice and approached her. Manjughosha understood that the Rishi's mind was distracted so she also put her Veena down and went closer. They both got so lost in each other that they didn't even notice the day and night. They started living together and many years passed like that. One day Manjughosha sought permission to return to her home in 'Dev-Lok (heaven)'. Rishi Medhavi told her to wait till the next morning but she denied that and said, "Rishivar! You are not aware but I have spent many years with you! please think about it and let me go."

Maharshi Lomesh told king Mandhata that after listening to Manjugosha, Rishi Medhavi was shocked, he realized that 57 years were already over, and in those years, he had completely forgotten his 'Tapasya' and only remained attached to physical pleasures. The virtues of the prior 'Tapasya' were also destroyed. He understood that Manjughosha was here to break his 'Tapasya'. The sage got angry and cursed her, "now you will be a vampire and live a miserable life. Manjugosha got upset after listening to this, still, she requested him humbly:

"Munivar! I know what I did was wrong but you know that when we come in a contact with a good person even for a short time it creates a great impact whereas I have spent 57 years with a great man like you and yet if I will degrade in 'Pishach yoni' then your greatness is worthless in front of the world. So please forgive me and reverse your curse, or show me a way to free myself from the curse. "Hearing this Rishi's anger subsided and said, "Devi Manjughosha! I will not be able to reverse my curse but if you will observe the papmochini Ekadashi Vrat which is coming in the waning Fortnite of Fagan months, you will be free from all your sins and my curse." On hearing this she bowed to Rishi Medhavi and Rishi left from there. He went to his father ChyavanMuni's ashram and narrated the incident with a sad heart. He said, "Dear Father! I have made a great mistake, please show me some atonement for this." ChyavanMuni suggested he observe the papmochini i.e. Fagan month's waning Fortnite Ekadashi Vrat and said if you observe this Vrat with true devotion your all sins will be destroyed.

Rishi Medhavi and Manjugosha both observe this Vrat and Worshipped Lord Vishnu. As a result, they were freed from their sins. Manjughosha was freed also from 'Pishach yoni' And again became a beautiful Apsara and went back to heaven.

View and significance as per Pushti sampradaya

The final destination of all souls i.e., 'Jivatmas' is to attain God -ultimate eternal happiness. The soul which is separated from God can have qualities of 'SAT' and 'CHIT' means knowledge about God and soul, but due to contact with the material world 'Jivatma' remains engaged in physical and material happiness. He forgot his true identity and lost the ultimate eternal happiness. When 'Jivatma' experiences complete peace of mind, he will easily be able to remain attached to God and get rid of his sins. Many people freed themselves from their sins after following Pushti sampradaya which was established by Shri Mahaprabhuji and after becoming true devotees of Shri Gusaiji. And that is why this Ekadashi is known as papmochini Ekadashi in Pushti sampradaya.

Views as per Maryada Path

According to the Bhavishya Purana Rishi Medhavi and Manjugosha observes the papmochini Ekadashi Vrat as per Chyavanmuni's advice and are freed from their sins.

Offerings to Lord Vishnu:

Charoli seeds are supposed to be offered to Lord Vishnu on this day.

Benefits:

If one observes Ekadashi Vrat will get freed from all sins and proximity of evil powers, and one can become Master of Ashta Siddhi.

Aarti

Jay Jay papmochini Ekadashi,

Jay papmochini Ekadashi

Fagan Maas ma malti,

Krishna Paksha ma falti,

Muni Shri Medhavi e Ekadashi Vrat karyu,

sarva papothi mukta thaya,

Apsara Manjughosha e Ekadashi Vrat karyu,

pishach deh thi mukta thaya

........Jay Jay

Sarva papo no nash karti,

Pishach Shakti no naash karti

Chamatkari Siddhi o aapti,

atiyant mangal kari

........Jay Jay

*****

11) Kamada Ekadashi

Kamada Ekadashi - Chaitra sud- Shukla paksha /waxing phase.

The importance of this Ekadashi is narrated by Lord Shri Krishna to King Yudhishthir.

Lord Sri Krishna said: "The eleventh tithi of waxing fortnight in Chaitra month is known as Kamada Ekadashi."

Ekadashi story

This story is from religious texts Purana and about King Pundrik, Gandharva Lalit, and Apsara Lalita. Rishi Vashishth had told this story to King Dilip.

King Pundarik of the Naga dynasty was ruling the Kingdom named Bhogawati.

He was such a powerful king that all Gandharvas, Yaksha, Kinnar, and Apsaras were serving him. A Gandharv couple named Lalit and Lalita was staying in his Kingdom.

They both had great love and respect for each other. They both were always attached. Once Lalit was performing music in king Pundrik's court, between which Lalita's thoughts distracted him so he started making mistakes in singing. A Naga named Karkotak became aware of the situation and informed the king about it. Hearing this, king Pundrik got angry and cursed him to be a demon. Immediately Lalit turned into a giant demon, with black skin and red eyes. The mere sight of him scared others. He ran away to the forest and ate whatever was found along the way. When Lalita saw this, she became very sad and started roaming behind her husband to get his original Gandharva form back.

Wandering around they both reached the Vindhyachal mountain. Rishi Rishyashrung was residing on this mountain. Lalit and Lalita went to the ashram and bowed down to Rishi with devotion. They told Rishi about the king's curse and their sufferings due to that. Rishi Rishyashrung was very kind and generous; he suggested that they should observe Chaitra Sukla Ekadashi which is known as Kamada Ekadashi Vrat. When Kamada Ekadashi day came they both observed Vrat with true devotion.

They worshipped Lord Vishnu and offered the virtue of Ekadashi fast to him. Due to that Lalit regained his original form with a divine aura and looked even better than earlier.

Lalita also became very beautiful due to the influence of the Ekadashi virtues. They both returned to their town. The King was pleased to see them again and reinstated Lalit to his service.

<u>**Views and significance according to Pushti Sampraday**</u>

Shri Yagnanarayan was a family member of Laxman bhattji. He wished to perform a hundred Som Yagnas and started with it. Laxman bhattji also performed five yagnas as a family member. His last yagna was on Kamada Ekadashi day, during yagna Lord appeared from the fire of 'Havana Kund ' and blessed them that he shall be born as Laxman bhattji's son, and Shri Mahaprabhuji born as Shri Laxman bhattji's son. That is why this day has great importance in Pushti Sampraday

<u>**Offering to Lord Vishnu**</u>

Clove is supposed to be offered on this day.

<u>**Benefits**</u>

One who observes this Vrat gets rid of the sins like brahmahatya gets freed from the curse and gets the assurance of male child.

<u>**Aarti**</u>

Jay Kamada Ekadashi,

Jay Jay Kamada Ekadashi.

Chaitra maase e ave,

Shukla paksha ma e fave

Putra prapti karave,

papothi e bachave......Jay

Rakshs yoni thi bachave,

roop sundar tu karave

Sukh shanti ne apave,

Aanand ne vistare....Jay

Vrat Ekadashi karu chhe,

Kamda taaru naam dharyu chhe

Hraday mahi stapee didha,

mukhthi taaru naam saryu chhe...Jay

Jay Jay Kamada Ekadashi.

*****

12) Varuthini Ekadashi

<u>Varuthini Ekadashi -</u> Chaitra vad- Krishna Paksha/ waning phase.

Lord Krishna has explained the significance of this Ekadashi to the king Yudhishthir, he said that the eleventh tithi of Chaitra month's waning phase is known as Varuthini Ekadashi. It provides happiness and good fortune during one's life and after death. On this auspicious day, Lord Varah is to be worshipped to get rid of sins and hardship. This day is the Birthday of Shri Mahaprabhu Vallabhacharyaji and that is why in Pushti Sampraday it is celebrated as 'Shri Vallabhacharya Jayanti' or 'Shri Vallabhacharya Pragtyotsav'.

Story

Long ago there was a king named Mandhata and his kingdom was situated on the banks of the river Narmada. The king was very pious and generous, his approach and acts were also very religious. Once he was doing 'Tapasya' (penance) in the forest.

When he was in deep meditation a wild bear came near him and started eating his legs. The king was very brave so he didn't get scared but distracted and remained seated for Tapasya. After chewing the king's legs for some time, the bear dragged him deep inside the forest. Now the king was scared and wanted to be free from the bear's clutches but his consciousness was not ready to kill the animal (bear) so he didn't react but started praying to Lord Vishnu and seeking his help.

Lord Vishnu is always ready to help his true devotees and that is why one of his names is 'Bhakt-vatsal'. After listening to King Mandhata's call the Lord appeared in front of him and killed the wild bear with his Sudarshan chakra. Lord also noticed that the king was unhappy because his legs were crumbled and eaten by the bear so, he condoles him and said, "don't worry my child, you go to Mathura city, observe the Varuthini Ekadashi Vrat and worship the statue of my Varah incarnation. Due to the virtue of these, you will regain your legs and you will be strong as before. What you suffered now was a result of your previous birth's crimes."

King Mandhata obeyed Lord's command exactly as he said and as result, his body was without any deformities and strong.

Views and significance according to Pushti Sampraday

Chaitra month is known as 'Madhav' month in the Sanskrit language. Word 'Ma' in Madhav resembles the goddess Laxmi and the word 'have' stands for the husband of Laxmi Devi. So, this month is considered Lord Vishnu's month. Shri Mahaprabhu Vallabhacharya, who established Pushti Sampraday, and Pushti devotees considered him as a partial incarnation was born on this day. Varuthini means who gives blessings, so pusti devotees believe that the Lord took birth in his month to bless them with His Leelas.

Maryada path views

Vishnu Purana shows that charity (Dana) of cows and education or knowledge (Vidyadhan) is considered as best on this auspicious day.

Offerings to Lord Vishnu

Muskmelon is supposed to be offered to the Lord on this day.

Benefits

One who observes this Vrat his all sins will be destroyed and always remain happy apart from that he will get the virtue of ten thousand years of Tapasya. This Vrat is also done for avoiding physical injuries and for the longevity of children's life.

Aarti

Jay Varuthini Ekadashi,

Jay Jay Varuthini Ekadashi

Chaitra mahine ave,

Krishna Paksha ma vrat karave

Saubhagya aapnari,

fal ni prapti lave....

Jay Varuthini Ekadashi

Sahastra Varsh ni Tapasya,

Ek upvas ma vasya

Swarag Ni prapti thaye,

Sukh ma tame hasya....

Jay Varuthini Ekadashi.

Vrat Ekadashi falya saune,

Ma Amla mallya saune

Harkhaya sahujano juo,

Hridaye ena dharya saune......

Jay Varuthini Ekadashi.

*****

13) Mohini Ekadashi

Mohini Ekadashi: Vaishakh sud - Sukla paksha/ waxing phase.

Why is this day known as Mohini Ekadashi?

Pandit Ganesh Mishra a noted astrologer of Kashi says that as per 'Vaishnava khanda' of 'Skanda Purana' Amruta originated from 'Samudra Manthan'. On this auspicious day, on the next day is on Baras tithi the Lord Vishnu had taken the form of Mohini for the protection of Amrut from the demons and on teras tithi, the Lord served Amrut to the Devtas for consumption. After consuming Amrut Devtas became powerful, they defeated demons on the fourteenth tithi and regained their kingdom on full moon day.

The significance of this day is described by Lord Shri Krishna to king Yudhishthir.

And before that Rishi Vashishth had told Shri Ram because Shri Ram wanted to listen about such a genuine Vrat which is considered superior among other Vrats and after observing it all kinds of problems should be dissolved and all sins should get destroyed.

Story

There was a beautiful town named Bhadravati on the banks of the river Saraswati. King Dhritiman was ruling there. He was very honest and pious and belonged to the 'Chandravansh' clan. A wealthy and affluent 'Vaishya' (caste who did business as per caste classification) named Dhanpal stayed in Bhadravati, whose name suggested his rich position. He was kind-hearted and a supreme devotee of Lord Vishnu. He was spending a lot of his wealth for the welfare of society and always remained engaged in philanthropy. He had made many wells, stepwell, lakes, schools, gardens, hospitals, and houses for poor people in the town. He had five sons. Sumati, Kirtibuddhi, Medhavi, Sukrut, and Dhrushtabuddhi. Their names were following their character, among them, Dhrushtabuddhi had many bad habits. He remained busy spending his father's money on adulterous activities like gambling and prostitution. He had no interest in business or virtuous activities like chanting holy names, worshiping the Lord, or showing respect towards Brahmins. Once he kept his hands around the neck of a prostitute and was openly roaming in the town. His father and brothers became angry at him and expelled him from their house. Now he had no money so it became difficult for him to meet his daily needs. He wandered around in grief and pain. over some time one day due to the influence of past virtues he reached the ashram of Maharishi Kaundinya. It was the hot summer of Vaishakh month. The Rishi arrived after a holy bath in the sacred river Ganga. Dhrushtabuddhi stood in front of him, he was feeling guilty, he asked the sage to show him a way or any Vrat which could free him from his nomadic life. Maharishi Kaundinya suggested that he must observe the Vrat of Mohini Ekadashi.

Muni Vashishth told Shri Ram that Dhrushtabuddhi was pleased with the suggestion and immediately followed it as per all rituals, due to the Vrat his all sins were destroyed and he became impeccable. He also got a divine body and attained Vaikuntha Dham by riding on a Garuda.

Views and significance according to Pushti Sampraday

Devtas and demons jointly did 'Samudra Manthan' to achieve 'Amrut' (divine nectar after consuming it one becomes immortal). When it appeared, Devtas and demons started quarreling about who will consume it first so Lord Vishnu took Mohini form and kept 'Amrut Kumbh' with him. That day was Fagan Shukla Ekadashi so this Ekadashi is known as Mohini Ekadashi. This incident is written in the Shrimad Bhagwat.

Views as per Maryada Path

After Seeta Mata left Ayodhya, Shri Ram missed her a lot. He told Muni Vashishth to show him such Vrat that one gets peace of mind, earns virtues, gets rid of physical pains, and his sins get destroyed after observing it and the sage told him to do Mohini Ekadashi Vrat.

Offering to Lord Vishnu.

Buttermilk should be offered to Lord Vishnu on this day.

<u>**Benefits**</u>

Those who read or listen to this story get the virtue of donating a thousand cows and for those who observe it, all his sins including past lives get destroyed.

<u>**Aarti**</u>

Jay Mohini Ekadashi.

Jay Jay Mohini Ekadashi

Vaishkh maas ma pratishtha,

Shukla paksha ma Punya ditha

Manuj janam safal thay,

fal eva te didha

..........Jay Mohini Ekadashi

Dhrutman ne bachavyo,

papmathi Ugaryo

Vishnu lok ne pamyo,

aanand sukh pamyo

........Jay Mohini Ekadashi

Vrat Mohini no saar chhe,

E Swarg nu ek dwar chhe

Sukhethi rahe jagma,

vrat no e vistar chhe.

.......Jay Mohini Ekadashi

*****

14) Apra Ekadashi

<u>Apra or Achla Ekadashi:</u> - Vaishakh Vad or Krishna Paksha/waning phase.

Apara Ekadashi is considered a sunray for destroying the darkness of sins.

One should observe this Vrat with devotion to attain Vaikuntha Dham.

Lord Shri Krishna has explained the significance of this Ekadashi to king Yudhishthir.

<u>**Story**</u>

The importance and detailed explanation of this Vrat is given in the Purana. According to the Padma Purana after doing this Vrat one's soul will never degrade to be a ghoul (Pret yoni). The other name of this day is Achla Ekadashi. Long ago there was a king named Mohidhwaj, he was very religious and ruled the Kingdom accordingly. His younger brother was a sinner and treacherous. Once he killed his elder brother and buried him under the peepal tree deep inside the forest. The untimely death of the king leads him to the ghostly matrix (Pret yoni). The king's soul as 'Bhoot' started residing on the peepal tree and began harassing passersby. One day a very wise and powerful Rishi Dhomya was passing through the way. When he saw the 'bhoot' he became aware of what had happened. The sage decided to free the king's soul. With the divine power of his knowledge, he brought down the ghost from the tree. He imparted knowledge of the afterlife and enlightened the king's soul. Incidentally, that was the day of Apra Ekadashi and the sage had observed a fast. The Rishi also passed on that virtue to the king. The king's soul was immediately freed from the ghostly matrix because of the collective power of knowledge and virtue. The soul gained a divine body and went to heaven.

A person who does things that are highly reprehensible like Brahmhatya, Even a man who kills Brahman, cows, and an unborn child, slanders and keeps relations with married women should be able to be free from all sins if he observes this, Vrat.

A person who cheats in his work fields either as a businessman or as an ayurvedic doctor, disciples who condemned his teacher (Guru) after gaining knowledge, a person who works as an astrologer without any knowledge of astrology, and a soldier (Kshatriya) who runs away from the battlefield all these leads to hell after death. Yet, the virtue of this Vrat is so influential that one can free himself by doing it.

<u>Views and significance according to Pushti Sampraday</u>

Apra word in Sanskrit is made from two words A (अ) and para (परा), where A(अ) means 'demonic' and para (परा) means 'own world'. To understand the difference between one's own and demonic views the Lord created two worlds daivee and Asuri (Worlds of Devtas and demons). The Lord's true devotees reside in the daivee world whereas souls (jivatma) who always remain attached to physical and material happiness (Maya) reside in the demonic world. The Lord loves their true devotees.

This thought is demonstrated in Pushti-Marg for Apra Ekadashi.

<u>Small poem on Apra Ekadashi</u>

Daivee Asuri be upjavi,

Prabhu man Kari vichar

Tema paheli nakhshikh sundari,

Shri hari ne manbhavi,

Biji katakshe je jan upna,

Maya ma thya leen,

Karma jad Asur anya bhajan dharam thi heen.

Views according to Maryada Path

Apra Ekadashi has great values, Brahmanda Purana says that this Vrat has the power to destroy all sins and also provide several virtues.

Offerings to Lord Vishnu

Cucumbers are offered to Lord Vishnu on this auspicious day.

Benefits

One who observes this Vrat and worships the Lord Vaman on this day will be free from all sins and attain Vaikuntha Dham. The virtue of reading or listening about this Vrat is equivalent to charity (dana) of a thousand cows.

Aarti

Jay Apra Ekadashi,

Jay Jay Apra Ekadashi

Vaishakh maas e viraje,

krishna paksh ma tu gaaje,

Brahmahatya naash thaye,

Bhoot yoni jaaye

....................Jay Apra Ekadashi

Shishyo - ne labhkari,

saune sukh aapnari

Swrnadan sam punya fal tu e denari

.................Jay Apra Ekadashi.

Vrat Apra fali gayu,

sukh anokhu mali gayu,

Fal mallya jeevan kera,

Nayan maru zari gayu

................Jay Apra Ekadashi.

*****

15) Nirjala Ekadashi

<u>Nirjala, Pandav or Bheem Ekadashi-</u> Jyeshtha Sud / Shukla paksha/waxing phase.

Lord Shri Krishna said to King Yudhishthir, "Maharishi Ved Vyas is Very learned and religious. He has great knowledge of the Vedas and all other religious texts, so he will tell you the significance of Nirjala Ekadashi."

Story

The Maharishi Ved Vyas said: "one should not have to consume any food on the eleventh tithi of each fortnight and on the following day after holy bath one has to worship Lord Vishnu and before completing fast one has to feed Brahmins. King! One should fast even in the days of 'Varadhi' (birth in the immediate family) and 'Sutak' (death in the immediate family)."

The younger brother of king Yudhishthir, Prince Bheem was also listening to this. He asked the Maharishi, "In my family, Kunta mata, and all my brothers King Yudhishthir, Arjun, Nakul, and Sahdev have regularly observed this Vrat and advised me for the same but my problem is that I can't bear hunger. The fire named 'Vruk' always remains active in my stomach and it cools only if I eat heavy meals. I can't skip a single meal of the day. "The Maharishi replied to Prince Bheem that if you wish to attain heaven after death you must observe all Ekadashi Vrat. On this, Prince Bheem agreed to only one fast in a year and asked Maharishi to suggest to him only fast which has the most virtues and is extremely beneficial for him."

Maharishi tells him that all of the merits achieved by fasting on all Ekadashi in a year can be attained by fasting on the one Nirjala Ekadashi. "Without drinking even water you should fast on the Ekadashi that occurs during the light Fortnite of the month of Jyeshtha (May- June) when the Sun travels in the sign of Taurus (Vrishabh)or Gemini (Mithun). Water can be used only for 'gargles' and 'Achaman' (is an intake of a sip of water before a Yagya or Puja,) apart from that any type of water consumption from Ekadashi Sunrise till next sunrise will break the fast. Whoever observes this Ekadashi should take a holy bath, give charity of water and gold to Brahmins or worthy persons on the next day which is baras tithi day, and only then should complete the fast. One has to Worship Lord Vishnu on this day. Another advantage of this Vrat is, that at the time of death the soul of such a person is not taken away by gigantic, monstrous, and ugly agents of Yamraj known as Yamdtutas but by the cool and calm agents of Lord Vishnu, known as Parshada, and placed in Vaikuntha Dham. The Vaysmuni added, Lord Krishna has told me that those who observe Nirjala (without water) fast and become my devotee will be free from all the sins."

After listening to Maharishi Prince Bheem started observing this Vrat and from that onwards this Ekadashi is known as Bheem, Pandav, or Nirjala Ekadashi.

Views and significance according to Pushti Sampraday

This Ekadashi is known as Nirjala because consumption of water is also restricted during this fast.

Prince Bheem also fasted accordingly but once he had water from the sacred river Shri Yamunaji under the direction of Lord Krishna. Vaishnava devotees can also consume the water of the Shri Yamuna River during the fast.

Views according to Maryada path

Religious text Padma Puran has described the significance of Nirjala Ekadashi. If one is not able to fast on all Ekadashis they can earn the virtues of all Ekadashi by fasting on this day.

Offerings to Lord Vishnu

Mangoes are to be offered to Lord Vishnu on this day.

Benefits

Those who listen or read about this Ekadashi Vrat and story will get the virtue of serving ancestors on no moon day. Their all sins will be destroyed and they will attain Vaikuntha Dham.

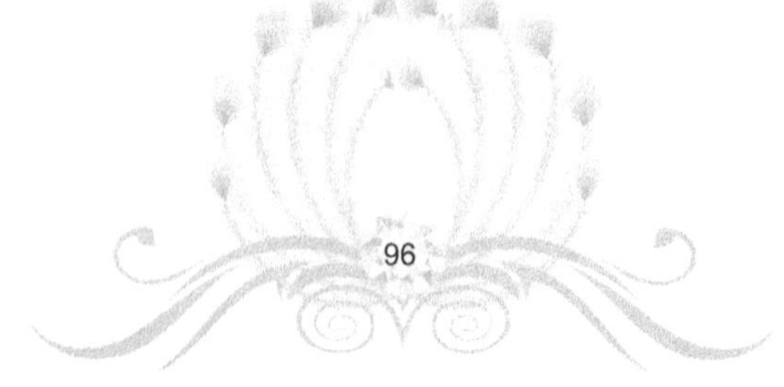

<u>**Aarti**</u>

Jay Nirjala Ekadashi,

Jay Jay Nirjala Ekadashi.

Jyeshtha maas ma e nyari,

Shukla paksha chhe Pyari,

Pandavo ni hitkari,

swarg ni adhikari

........Jay Nirjala Ekadashi

Vishnu puja sau karta,

gaudaan pan falta

Katha je koi sambde,

punya karodo malta

.............Jay Nirjala Ekadashi

Aa jeevan sawari didhu,

Avu kaam Nirjala e kidhu,

Unchu pad apavyu amne,

Dukhdu te hari lidhu.

..........Jay Nirjala Ekadashi

*****

16) Yogini Ekadashi

<u>Yogini Ekadashi:</u> - Jyeshtha Vad- Krishna Paksha/ waning phase.

Lord Shri Krishna told King Yudhishthir, "The eleventh tithi of Jyeshtha month's waning phase is known as Yogini Ekadashi." And also described the significance of this day.

<u>Story:</u>

Kuber, the king of the heavenly kingdom alkapuri was a great devotee of Lord Shiva. Every Morning he worshipped the Lord and performed the Puja of deity with flowers. Every day, a gardener named Hem fetched flowers from Mansarovar for king Kuber's puja. As per his daily routine Hem collected flowers but after going home, he got enticed by his wife Vishalakshi's beauty and lost complete control over himself. Here in the temple, the king expected him as per daily routine, but he didn't reach till noon, and puja time got over. The king became very angry about this and ordered his servant to call and enquire about his absence. When the king became aware of the reason, he lost his temper. As a punishment, the king cursed him, "You have insulted Lord Shiva, so now you will suffer from vitiligo skin disease and will get away from your wife" and expelled him from Alkapuri. Soon after facing the king's ire. He landed on earth with vitiligo skin and separated from his wife. The Hem was also a devotee of Lord Shiva so he didn't lose his memory after cursing. He wandered in the forest in search of food and water and felt guilty for offending the king. While wandering they reached a mountain peak named Meru Giri. Here accidentally he met the great sage, Markandeya Muni. He bowed down to Muni, narrated the incident, and sought his advice. He was guilty of his deed and was shivering due to fear. The Sage appreciates his truth and condoled him. He advised him to observe the Vrat of Yogini Ekadashi.

In continuing the story Lord Shri Krishna told king Yudhishthir that Hem followed Markandeya Muni's advice with true devotion and due to that he was freed from vitiligo disease and remained happy ever after.

<u>Views and significance according to Pushti Sampraday</u>

One of the great disciples of Shri Mahaprabhu Vallabhacharya and the 'Ashta sakha'.

Kumbhandas was 'Param Bhakt' (true devotee) of Lord Shrinathji. Apart from that, he was also a great singer and musician of that era. He had such great devotion that he was able to attain yog samadhi (deeply concentrate on the Lord and forget the outer world completely) during the Seva. He attains Yog samadhi on Yogini Ekadashi Day.

Views according to Maryada path

The significance of Yogini Ekadashi is found in Brahma Vaivarta Purana. Lord Krishna has explained the importance of this Ekadashi to king Yudhisthira and Markandeya Muni has explained the story of the Vrat and its rituals to the Yaksha community.   The Yogini word 'is made up of two words, Yogi means Lord Shankar and 'Ni' means Dev Parvati. Once on Yogini Ekadashi Day Lord Shiva and Devi Parvati did a night awakening (Ratri Jagran). They both discussed the Brahma Raat (night of Lord Brahma) and the Vishnu Raat (night of Lord Vishnu) on that night. and in that discussion, they talked about this auspicious day also.

Offerings to Lord Vishnu

Sugar is to be offered to Lord Vishnu on this day.

Benefits

Those who observe this Vrat will get the virtue of giving a meal to eighty-eight thousand Brahmins. Those who listen or read about this story will get rid of all the sins.

Aarti

Jay Yogini Ekadashi,

Jay Jay Yogini Ekadashi

Jyeshtha mahine chhalkave,

Krishna paksha ma dodi ave

Dharamraj ne batavee,

Krishna ene laave re

...........Jay Jay Yogini Ekadashi

Hemmali sharan taare avyo,

Kuber na shrap thi bachavyo,

Kodh nivaryo

...........Jay Jay Yogini Ekadashi

Vrat Yogini kare j koi,

Hriday mata dhare Je koi

Eno udhhar nakki,

Yogini Vrat aj fale sau hoi

...........Jay Yogini Ekadashi.

*****

17) Devshayani Ekadashi

<u>Devshayani, Devpodhi or Padma Ekadashi</u> - Ashadh sud Shukla paksha/waxing phase.

<u>Why is this Ekadashi known as Devshayani or Devpodhi Ekadashi?</u>

Dev podhi Ekadashi is a day, from that onwards one form of Lord Shri Krishna resides in Patal lok at the gates of king Bali's court, and his other form rest in the Cosmic Milk Ocean (kshirsagar) on the bed of Shesha naga for four months or till the Devuthi Ekadashi. There is also another story that Lord Shri Krishna gets very tired during the war with the demon 'Shankhasur', So, after killing the demon he rests for four months in Patal Lok.

Generally, these are the months of the monsoon season and these four months are known as Chaturmas. In olden times it was very difficult to travel during this season due to lack of transport facilities. In today's time, the situation is better but yet not advisable for long walking journeys. That is the reason that Saints, Sadhu, and Muni's stopped their pilgrimage and lived only at one place during the Chaturmas. You can also say that holy places became a standstill on Chaturmas. Vaishnava devotees believe that all pilgrimage places gather in Vraj during that time and that is why all other pilgrimage places except the Vraj region remain closed on chaturmas. On Devshayani Ekadashi day Vaishnav devotees organize Mathura Vrindavan parikrama (walking across the holy places in Mathura). Varaha Purana has nicely explained the significance of this parikrama. Chaturmash vrat (taking any vrat regarding food patterns like eating, once in a day or giving up particular food items like onion, garlic, or bread.) Those who wish for Moksha free from the repetitive cycle of birth and death) should also start with any Chaturmas vrat / Vishnu - Shayan vrat from this day.

According to the Skanda Purana, all devatas and all pilgrimages take asylum at Lord Vishnu's feet, that is why those who worship and do puja of Lord Vishnu their life became blessed. The Lord rests during chaturmas in the ocean and that is why holy baths also have great virtues during this time. The significance and story of this Ekadashi are described by Lord Shri Krishna to the king Yudhishthir. The Lord also told him the Ekadashi story which was earlier told by Lord Brahma to Narad Muni.

Ekadashi story.

Long ago there was a 'Suryavanshi' (sun clan) king named Mandhata, he was not only truthful and pious but also a savior of cows and brahmins. His subjects were very happy with his reign. Once there was a drought for three consequent years in his Kingdom. All food stocks were depleted, and people and animals were dying from hunger.

Parents could not bear the sight of their starving children. Looking at the scenario, king Mandhata thought that surely due to some of my faults my kingdom is suffering from the drought. To find a solution he went to Maharishi Angiras. The Maharshi suggested that he and his subjects should have to observe the Devshayani Ekadashi fast. He said that this Vrat is extremely beneficial for society, it will definitely fulfill all your wishes and will also destroy all types of suffering and pain. The King and his subjects immediately follow the advice of the Maharishi and observe the Vrat. Soon rain started and mother earth flourished again. People danced with joy, the animals survived and farmers became very happy to see that the new crop will grow again and that happened also.

Views and significance according to Pushti Sampraday

The emotions of missing Lord Krishna by Vrajnaris or gopikas (women of the Vraj region) are the predominant factor of this day in pushti marg. Lord Shri Krishna was staying in Gokul and did many Leelas on the bank of the Yamuna river and across Vraj during his childhood. He went to Mathura on this Ekadashi day and from that onwards they felt lonely. During this monsoon season, all vrajnaris were eagerly waiting for Lord Shri Krishna to return and remembering the time which they had spent happily with him.

They were thinking about why we get attracted to the Lord when we look at him! And what Lord sees in us is that he made us his friend (Sakhi).

A close friend of Lord Shri Krishna named 'Padmasakhi' was remembering 'panghat leela' (activities and fun they had on the banks of river Yamuna).

<u>**Offerings to Lord Vishnu**</u>

Grapes are to be offered to the Lord on this day.

<u>**Benefits**</u>

This Vrat pleased Lord Vishnu. It also provides devotion and liberation so everyone must observe this, Vrat.

<u>**Aarti**</u>

Jay Devshayani Ekadashi,

Jay Jay Devshayani Ekadashi

Ashdh maasma falti,

Shukla paksha ma dukh harti

Mandhata raj ne taaryo,

daya krupa zarti

...............Jay Jay Padma Ekadashi

Vrat Devshayani nyaru,

devo manvo ne chhe pyaru

Fale antar dharta ene,

thay saghde saaru.

...............Jay Jay Ekadashi

*****

18) Kamika Ekadashi

Kamika Ekadashi: - Ashadh Vad - Krishna Paksha/ waning phase.

The significance of this Ekadashi is described by Lord Shri Krishna to king Yudhisthira. He said, "I will tell you a story which Lord Brahma had told Narad Muni when he asked about that."

Ekadashi story

Shri Narad Muni asked Lord Brahma, O Lord, please tell me about the waning phase Ekadashi of Ashadh month. The Lord Brahma replied, "Maharshi, please listen carefully, to what I am telling you because these answers are not only for you but also for the welfare of the entire Mankind. This Ekadashi is known as "Kamika" Ekadashi. One should worship Lord Vishnu on this day. This day is so sacred that even if one just listens about this vrat he will get the virtue of Vaajpey Yagya. "Charity (dana) of gold and land is considered the most virtuous according to religious beliefs. It is said that those who do charity of these things will attain Moksha and in case he gets a rebirth he will receive a lot of wealth and land. Now the question is, how can a poor man collect this virtue because he doesn't have either gold or land! As an answer, Padma Purana suggests that if one will observe the kamika Ekadashi vrat and worship Lord Vishnu with 'Tulsi Patra' he will get the virtue which is considered rare. His all sins will get destroyed and he will also attain the virtue of donating the land equivalent to the earth including water bodies and forests because Lord Vishnu loves 'Tulsi Patra'. He will be more pleased with it rather than gems like gold, pearl, or Ruby. This vrat is best for those who just remained engaged in the material pleasures and physical happiness. This vrat has more virtue than one collects by working for his spiritual upliftment. Every devotional activity which you perform on this day like Jagran (night awakening) chanting the holy name, puja with Tulsi seeds, that all have great virtues, their all sins get destroyed, after death, their soul will not be taken by Yamdtutas but by Vishnu Servants and they attain Vaikuntha Dham.

Long ago there lived a brave Kshatriya (one of the four Varna associated with warrior aristocracy) in a small village. One day due for some reason he got in a fight with a brahmin and the brahmin died. The Kshatriya felt guilty and wanted to perform the brahmins after the death ceremony. But pandits (brahmins who perform rituals of all pujas) didn't allow him to associate with the ceremony and other brahmins refused to have meals at his home because he had done Brahmahatya (murder of a Brahmin). And said, "First you complete atonement of this and get freed from sin only then we will accept food from your residence." The Kshatriya asked them which vrat shall he practice being free from his sin? At that time the Brahmins suggested he observe vrat of waning phase Ekadashi of Ashadh month, conducting Vishnu Pooja, and offering food to Brahmins on that day. He will be free from sin. The Kshatriya did accordingly and That night Lord Vishnu appeared in front of him and said now you are free from Brahmahatya.

Views and significance according to pushti sampradaya.

In the monsoon season, 'vrajnaris' (Kamika) were missing Lord Krishna. Just like it rains very heavily with thunder and lightning in the month of ashadh, the vrijnaris eyes were flowing with tears and bodies were shivering and they were longing to meet the Lord. They were praying to him, "Oh Lord, we are eager to meet you and waiting for you to come please do come fast".

Significance according to Maryada Path

Brahma vairvrat Puran has described the significance of Kamika Ekadashi. This significance was told by Lord Brahma to Narad Muni when he asked about it. After performing this Vrat when will get rid of all sins like 'brahmahataya' (killing brahmins) and 'gauhatya' (killing cow). Disorders that arise in the mind will also get destroyed and one will be pious.

Offerings to Lord Vishnu

Wheat is to be offered to Lord Vishnu on Kamika Ekadashi day.

Benefits

The one who does Ekadashi vrat will be free from all sins and attain Vaikuntha Dham even after doing a different kind of killing mankind.

<u>**Aarti**</u>

Kamika Ekadashi Aarti

Jay Jay Kamika Ekadashi,

Jay Jay Kamika Ekadashi,

Ashdh maase sukhdayi,

Krishna Paksha E faldayi,

Tulsi ni puja re,

chhe param Anandayee

...............Jay Jay Kamika Ekadashi

Ghee no divo zagmagto,

eno vansh sudhapan karto,

Suryalok ma farto,

sukh Shanti ne pamto

...............Jay Jay Kamika Ekadashi.

Vrat Kamika je koi kare,

Ena jeevan ma sukhdu thare,

Vishwase vahan tarshe,

evu kam mata kare

...............Jay Jay Kamika Ekadashi.

*****

19) Pavitra Ekadashi

<u>**Pavitra / Putrada Ekadashi:**</u> - Shravan sud - Shukla paksha / waxing phase.

The eleventh tithi of Shravan month's waxing fortnight is known as Pavitra Ekadashi. It is also known as Putrada Ekadashi. (Posh month's waxing phase Ekadashi is also known as Putrada Ekadashi). Lord Shri Krishna explained the importance of the Ekadashi to King Yudhishthira.

Story of Ekadashi

A long time ago, In the 'dwapar yuga' (Era in which Dharma stands on two pillars).

King Mahijeet was ruling The Kingdom of Mahishmati Puri. The king was happy in all manners but he didn't have an heir, so he was sad and worried about it. To find a solution to this he called his courtiers and sought their advice. The Brahmins in his court went to various very learned Rishimuni's ashrams for a solution. After a long search, they came into contact with 'Lomesh Muni'. The lifespan of Lomesh Muni is as long as Lord Brahma. When Lord Brahma's one 'Kalp' (approx 4.32 billion years) ends, one hair (known as loma) from Lomesh Muni's body falls. And that is why his name was Lomesh Muni. He was very learned and aware of the past, present, and future. Listening to them the Rishi sat in meditation and was able to see everything in the meditation and also understood the reason behind the king's problem. He opened his eyes and said, "In his previous birth the king was poor and deceitful. He was born in a Vaishya family (caste/varna associated with the business) who traveled from one village to another for his business deals. Once while traveling on Jyeshtha waxing Ekadashi day, he became thirsty and went near a Lake to drink water. He saw one thirsty cow with its newly born calf drinking water. Unable to control his thirst, he stopped them and had water, due to that he earned /collected sins, and because of those sins, he isn't able to have children at this birth. To get rid of this the king, his ministers, and his subjects should observe Shravan Shukla Ekadashi vrat. The reason why you along with the king should do this Vrat is to pass those virtues to the king and with the influence of that, he will surely be blessed with a child." Hearing this Brahmins returned to their kingdom and told this King Mahijeet. They all followed Lomesh Muni's advice, due to these the king's sins were destroyed and a beautiful prince took birth in his palace.

As per another story, this Ekadashi is known as Putrada Ekadashi because Ashta Sakha Kumbhandas Ji was born on Chaitra month's waning Ekadashi with a blessing to his father Bhagwandasji from a sage in the 'Kumbh Mela' of Prayag. Bhagwandasji received blessings on Shravana's putrada Ekadashi day.

Views and significance according to pushti sampradaya.

This day has a lot of significance in Pushti sampradaya and is known as Pavitra Ekadashi. This day is also known as the origin day of Pushti-marg. The Lord was born at midnight to remove three types of flaws in his devotees. These flaws are

Adhibhautika - of body

Adhyatmik - of soul

Adhidaivika - of Devtas

From ancient times devotees offer 'Pavitra Mala' to the Lord on this day.

During satyug they were made from gems, in treta Yug it was of gold, in dwapar Yug.

It was of silk thread and currently in Kalyug it is of cotton thread.

Once Shri Mahaprabhuji was wandering with Shri Damodardas Harsa (the first disciple of Shri Mahaprabhuji to whom he gave Brahma sambandh.) on the bank of river Yamuna. Shri Mahaprabhuji was missing the Lord eagerly and was anxious, as he was not sure when he would be able to do his 'Darshan' (able to see him). He was also worried about the spiritual upliftment of all jivatmas. Shrinathji was aware of the devotional mental condition of his true devotee so he appeared in front of him and blessed him.

The Lord said, "Vallabh! I know what you wish but currently, in this 'Kaliyuga' spiritual upliftment of jivatmas is not possible with Gyan, Karma, or Yoga (i.e., knowledge, work, or Meditation). Instead, if a jivatma will take my asylum I will surely save him. So, you give Brahma Sambandh to Pushti devotees. "And the Lord gave Brahma Sambandh Mamta to Shri Mahaprabhuji. As honor, Shri Mahaprabhuji offered a Pavitra Mala, which was made of cotton thread and colored with saffron to Lord Shrinathji. From that onwards the system of offering 'Pavitra Malas' to Lord and Guru on Ekadashi and Dwadashi day started. Cotton thread in a Pavitra Mala is a symbol of devotion and love towards the Lord. As the name suggests Pavitra means sacred and there is nothing as sacred as love. The cotton thread of the pavitra mala is like love. it is very fragile, once it is broken it is difficult to rejoin so it needs care. In the same manner, to maintain love and respect constantly it should be nourished with devotion. The saffron color is the symbol of 'Shri Swaminiji' (Shri Radha). Devotees offer saffron Pavitra Mala with the emotions of 'Shri Swaminiji'. Along with Pavitra Mala devotees also offer saffron sugars(mishri) to Lord.

Pavitra Malas are also made from silk thread, silk is very soft, just like love is also very soft so it is a symbol of the softness of the heart. 'Narad Bhakti Sutra' has been described as the softest. Pavitra Mala contains 360 threads when we offer it to the Lord, we are also offering soft and sacred feelings of our heart along with it. 360 threads of Pavitra are also a sign of offering feelings of Nitya Seva (daily service of 360 days). Pushti devotees also offered Pavitra Malas to the Guru of Shri Vallabhacharya clan and sometimes to other Vaishnavas. Many Vaishnav may offer Pavitra Mala to Lord instead of flower Mala.

Everyone has to offer Pavitra Mala to Lord as per their caste (Varnashrama) on Shravana's waxing phase Ekadashi day with sandals, flowers, kumkum, rice grains, and dhoop sticks. One can't offer during Shravani and Bhadra Nakshatra. Devotees also decorate the Backdrop, Lord's seat, and swing with Pavitra Malas. It can be offered any day till Janmashtami if one can't do that due to any reason, he can offer it till Prabodhini Ekadashi (Dev Diwali). It's a belief that if one will not offer Pavitra Mala to Lord then Nitya Seva will be meaningless and that is why it is a must for every Pushti devotee.

Significance according to Maryada path.

According to the Ramachhen Chandrika Granth, a Naga named 'Pavitra' was a younger brother of Vasuki naga. He did Tapasya for a hundred years and pleased Lord Shiva. When Lord Shiva asked for a boon, he said that he wanted a place around the Lord's neck. Lord agreed to that and said all brahmins and those Kshatriya who do daily puja will worship you in the month of Shravan and that day will be celebrated as an occasion changing their holy thread (Janoi) for all Ved Pathi (samvedi, yajurvedi, atharvavedi and rigvedi) brahmins.

Offerings to Lord Vishnu

Shingoda (Water chestnut) is to be offered to the Lord on this day.

Benefits

Those who observe this Vrat will get happiness in current and coming births.

Those who read or listen to this Ekadashi story will be blessed with children and their all sins get destroyed.

<u>**Aarti**</u>

Jay Putrada Ekadashi,

Jay Jay Putrada Ekadashi

Shravan paksha e falti,

Shukla paksha ma malti

Mahijeet raja sudhrya,

farya drashti karti.

...............Jay Jay Putrada Ekadashi

Putra prapti sanghe karave,

Vrat puja je dikhlave

Karya siddh thaye,

Marg satya batave.

...............Jay Jay Putrada Ekadashi

Vrat putrada evu faltu,

Santan sukh saune maltu

Killol kare angne re sukhdu nyaru dhartu

...................Jay Jay Ekadashi

*****

20) Aja Ekadashi

Aja or Anada Ekadashi: - Shravan vad - Krishna paksha/waning phase.

Lord Shri Krishna has explained the significance of this Ekadashi to king Yudhishthir. He said, "Waning phase Ekadashi of Shravan month is known as Anada or Aja Ekadashi. It is very sacred, those who perform this Vrat and worship Lord Vishnu on this day their all sins will be destroyed."

Ekadashi story

In the golden era, there was a very renowned king known as Harishchandra. He was a truthful and very pious king. The spread of his Kingdom was very vast. Due to some unknown reason and to maintain the dignity or keep the value of his own words he left his kingdom. He also sold his wife, son, and himself and worked as a slave to 'Chandala' (those who work in shamshan, burial sites) and his earning was only a cover cloth of a dead body. He faced many problems, yet he stuck to his words.

Many years passed like that but his condition didn't improve. Many times, he got worried about what to do to come out from this suffering! One day Maharishi Gautam was passing through there. He saw the king and the pain on his face, so he came near to the king. King immediately bowed down to the sage and narrated his painful story to him. Maharishi told him to observe the vrat with Jagran (night awakening) on the auspicious day of Anada Ekadashi which was just after seven days and said there is a lot of virtue in this sacred Vrat and those virtues will surely burn all your sins and you will be free from suffering. The king observed the vrat as the rishi had said, with the influence of that he was freed from all sufferings. His wife and son returned to him and he regained his kingdom. All Devtas welcomed him back with flowers raining on him with drum sounds from the sky. And he attained heaven with his family after death.

Views and significance according to Pushti Sampraday

According to the story in Shrimad Bhagwat, a Vaishnav named 'Ajamil' was a sinner. At the time of his death, he called his son 'Narayan' again and again.

Unknowingly, he called the Lord (Narayan is one of the names of Lord Vishnu) so the Lord was condescending to him and gave him Moksh. This day was of Shravan waning Ekadashi so this day is known as Aja Ekadashi.

According to Maryada Marg

In Brahmand Puran Vyas Muni has said that this Vrat is very sacred and provides happiness and wealth to all.

Offerings to Lord Vishnu

Dry dates (kharek) are to be offered to the Lord on this day.

<u>**Benefits**</u>

Those who observe this Vrat their all sins get destroyed and attain heaven and those who read or listen about this will get the virtue of Ashwamegh Yagya.

<u>**Aarti**</u>

Jay Jay Aja Ekadashi,

Jay Jay Aja Ekadashi,

Shravan Maas e pragte,

Krishna Paksha ma malke

Harishchandra ne bachvyo,

ek khan ne palke

.............Jay Jay Aja Ekadashi

Ratri Harigun thaye,

tema hari gun gaaye

Dev sthiti prapt thaye paap sarve jaaye

.............Jay Jay Aja Ekadashi

Vrat Aja evu shrdhhalu, astha kare Andhashraddha lu

Pad dev nu maltu,

thatu antare ajwalu

.............Jay Jay Aja Ekadashi.

*****

21) Vaman Ekadashi

<u>**Vaman, Jal zilani, dana or parivartini Ekadashi:**</u> -
Bhadrapad sud shukla / waxing phase ekadashi.

The significance of this Ekadashi is described by Lord Shri
Krishna to the king Yudhisthira. He said, "Dharmaraj, now I will
tell you about the waxing phase Ekadashi of Bhadrapad month
which has the power to destroy all sins and provide heaven after
death."

<u>**Ekadashi story**</u>

This Ekadashi has many different names. For those who
worship Lord Vishnu on this auspicious day, it is considered
that he worshipped all three Lords, Lord Brahma, Lord Vishnu,
and Lord Mahesh. I will provide him with the fruit of cosmic

worship. Observing this Vrat is equal to doing all types of Vrats and Pujas.

Vaman Ekadashi

Lord Krishna started with the story, Long back in 'Treta Yug' there was a king named Bali, king of demons. Even though he was a demon, he was a great devotee of mine and regularly performed Yagna, Puja, Havan, and Penance. He achieved the Kingdom of heaven with his devotional powers and that is why Devtas were considering him his enemy. All Devtas requested me to free heaven from his rule and that is why I had to con him by taking the Vaman incarnation.

As a Vaman Brahmin (Small Brahmin) I went to his court and asked for three steps of land as 'Bhiksha' to which he agreed immediately. I changed my form from Vaman (small) to Virat (gigantic). My shape was so huge that it covered the whole cosmos. (All lokas) Every devta started worshipping me after looking at my huge form. In my first step, I covered the whole earth and in my second step, I covered heaven. Now no place was left so I asked him, where shall I put my third step?

King Bali was surprised by this and recognized me. he bowed down to my feet and replied! "Oh Lord, please put your third step on my head." I put my leg on his head, pushed him in the 'Patal lok', and took off his pride. There he took my asylum and I blessed him that I will stay near you and from that day onwards one of my forms is always with him in patal lok and my other form is in milk ocean (kshirsagar). King Yudhishthira, I did this on the auspicious day of Bhadrapad.

Waxing Ekadashi so those who observe this Vrat or listen about this I give them the virtue of one thousand Ashwamegh yagyas.

Those who do charity(dana) of curd, rice grains, or silver attain heaven and their all sins get destroyed."

This Ekadashi is also known as Jayanti Ekadashi. The baras tithi means the next day of Ekadashi is celebrated as Vaman Dwadashi.

Jal Zilani or Padma Ekadashi.

This day is also known as Jal Zilani Ekadashi day. It is written in religious texts that Lord Shri Krishna sailed to the river Yamuna with vrajgopikas on this day. From that onwards, this tradition is going on. The way all vraj gopikas completely surrender themselves to Lord Krishna, devotees should also surrender to 'God' and 'Guru', this is the intensive meaning of this Ekadashi.

Views and significance according to Pushti Sampraday Daan Ekadashi

The sales tax which is taken by the government was known as 'Jakat' 'Vero' or 'Daan' (in Gujarati) in olden times. Father of Lord Shri Krishna Nand Baba was the king of the Vraj region so Lord Krishna could ask for alms on sales of butter (Makhan), buttermilk, or curd at Mathura. Shri Thakorji (Shri Krishna) broke or grabbed the pots and made his friends and monkeys eat them. There is a deep intention behind this and other 'Leelas' like rasleela Man leela etc. of Lord Krishna, which one should try to understand. Lord also wished that jivatma gets closer to him.

<u>**Significance according to Maryada path Parivartini Ekadashi**</u>

On the Dev podhi Ekadashi day of Ashadh month Lord started resting in the Milk Ocean (Kshirsagar) and wakes up on Dev uthi Ekadashi day in Kartik month but on Bhadrapad Sud Ekadashi day he changes the sleeping position (turn around) and that is why this day is also celebrated as Parivartini Ekadashi.

<u>**Offerings to Lord Vishnu**</u>

Curd and cucumber are to be offered to Lord on this day.

<u>**Benefits**</u>

Those who observe this Vrat shall get the virtue of one thousand Ashwamegh Yagyas.

<u>**Aarti**</u>

Jay Jay Vaman Ekadashi,

Jay Vaman Ekadashi

Bhadarva ma pratishtha,

Shukla paksha ma Nishtha

Vaaman Rupe padharya,

Bali danav Savarya.........

Jay Jay Vaman Ekadashi

Shri Krishna karvat le,

saune Ashirvachan de,

Vaman tethi kahe,

Antarma Nit rahe.........

Jay Jay Ekadashi

Vrat Vaman ni Nyari,

ful divya na bhata kyari

Jay Samsya Vari Vari,

Ujade Duniya sari......

Jay Jay Ekadashi.

*****

22) Indira Ekadashi

Indira Ekadashi: - Bhadrapada vad / Krishna paksha / Waning phase.

Lord said: The eleventh tithi of the Bhadrapada month's Waning phase is known as Indira Ekadashi. This Vrat destroys all the sins and uplifts the souls of ancestors who suffer in hell.

Story of Ekadashi

In the Satyug era, there was a benevolent and renowned King named Indrasen. He was a great devotee of Lord Vishnu and spent most of his time in worship and devotional services. While performing daily activities also he ruminates on the thoughts of spiritual upliftment. Once Devrishi Narad entered his palace by way of the sky. The king warmly welcomed him and did his puja.

The king said, "Munivar my kingdom became sacred with your sanctified feet and your presence, please tell me what can I do for you?" On that Nardmuni said, "Oh king! You might be surprised by my words, but your father is in Yama Loka. I saw him when I was there and he had sent a message to you that due to the sin of breaking the Vrat, which he had committed during his lifetime, he is suffering in Yamaloka. He wants to attain heaven and for that reason, he had told you to observe Indira Ekadashi fast and pass its virtue to him, with the influence of those virtues he will attain heaven. Now I will tell you how to do this Vrat. On the previous day of Ekadashi (Dasam tithi), you have to take a Holy bath and consume food only once at noon.

At night you have to sleep on the ground and on Ekadashi day after brushing and bathing you have to start fast. At noon you need to perform 'Shradha puja' (a ritual for homage to ancestors) for your forefathers in front of the shaligram. You have to smell the 'pind' (food lump) of Shradh puja and feed that to the cow. Give Dakshina (charity) to brahmins and feed them. At night you do 'Jagran' (night awakening) while chanting the holy name, the next day (baras tithi) after worshipping Lord Vishnu and keeping 'maun' (not to speak) you have to dine with your family. Indrasen, if you will do this Vrat Puja with the true devotion your forefathers will surely attain Vaikuntha Dham."

After narrating this Narad Muni went back to heaven and the King followed his advice with all his wives, sons, and brothers. After Vrat all Devtas from the sky shower them with flowers and Indrasen's father goes to Vaikuntha Dham on Garuda (vehicle of Lord Vishnu). Later he passed the throne to his son and went to heaven after his demise.

Views and significance according to pushti sampradaya

As per Brahma Vaivarta Purana when Lord Vishnu was born as Shri Krishna in Gokul as a son of Nand baba and Yashoda Maiya at that time Shri Mahalaxmi Devi went to Vraj for doing 'Darshan' of Lord. But it was very difficult for her because the Lord was surrounded by Gopa and Gopis. With the intention of Nitya darshan (daily seva), Lord Laxmiji became enthroned in Vraj.

It is written in Gopi geet;

जयति तेऽधिकं जन्मना व्रज:

श्रयत इन्दिरा शश्वदत्र हि।

Views as per Maryada path

There was a king named Indrasen in the Mahishmati Kingdom. His father broke the fast of Indira Ekadashi so he attained Yamaloka. On the advice of Narad Muni, king Indrasen observed Vrat along with his family and all rituals. With the influence of that virtues, his father attained Vaikuntha Dham, and over some time he also proceeded.

Offerings to Lord Vishnu

Jaggery and Ghee are to be offered to Lord on this day.

Benefits

Those who listen to or read about this Vrat story there all scenes get destroyed and they attain heaven after death.

<u>**Aarti**</u>

Jay Jay Indira Ekadashi,

Jay Jay Indira Ekadashi

Bhadarva maase harakhti,

Krushna paksha E Uchhalti

Indrasen ne taaryo,

Danav rup thi Savariyo.........

Jay Jay Indira Ekadashi

Raja rank swarg paame,

Ekadashi nu fal pame

Punyashali thay naame,

Devi khud ema Biraje.........

Jay Jay Indira Ekadashi

Vrat Indira dhare je re,

Eni iccha fale saue

Kare diwada chare kore,

din ena fare te re.........

Jay Jay Indira Ekadashi

*****

23) Pashakunsha Ekadashi

Pashakunsha Ekadashi- Ashwin (Aso) sud Shukla paksha/ waxing phase.

The significance of this Ekadashi is narrated by Lord Shri Krishna to the king Yudhishthira. He said, oh King! The eleventh tithi of the waxing phase of Ashwin (Aso) month is known as Pashakunsha Ekadashi.

Ekadashi story

The Lord continued; everyone has to perform the puja of the Lord Padma Nath (Lord Vishnu) on this auspicious day. This Ekadashi destroys all the sins and provides health, wealth, friends, a pious wife, heaven, and Moksha. Those who observe this fast during the day and 'Jagran' (night awakening) will never face Yamadutas at the time of death, instead attain Vaikuntha Dham with a divine form, ornaments, and pitambar. Such a noble person also saved ten maternal and paternal generations of his and his wife as they too shall benefit from the virtues of the vrat.

<u>Views and significance according to Pushti Sampraday: -</u>

Shri Gusaiji is very kind and generous; he accepts all his devotees as they are and tries to uplift them. With the divine grace of Shri Gusaiji, his devotees never face any problems whether they are physical, metaphysical, spiritual, or theological. He will not face any worldly problems which are generally written in destiny. Not only that but one can attain Moksha or be permanently placed at 'Gaulok Vraj Mandal' Nitya Leela sthan of Lord Shri Krishna. Shri Vitthalnath (Shri Gusaiji) was born with the wish of the Lord and for the upliftment of devotees and daivee jivas. Shri Gusaiji saved the 'Jivatmas' who had degraded due to the bad influence from the 'pass' which means rope of Yamraj to tie Jivatmas and 'kusha' means a weapon of Yamraj to punish jivatmas, (jointly known as pashakunsha) on this auspicious Ekadashi day and that is why this Ekadashi is known as pashakunsha Ekadashi.

<u>News according to Maryada Sampraday</u>

Those who spend their time in bad influence rather than devotional services like Dan(charity) Darshan, or bhajans go to hell after death. As Lord Shri Krishna has described in Brahmanda Purana about this Ekadashi all problems get resolved and they attain permanent happiness by observing this, Vrat.

<u>Offerings to Lord Vishnu</u>

Muskmelons are to be offered to the Lord on this day.

Benefits

Those who observe this Vrat will get devotion towards Lord but indirectly he will gain fame and wealth.

Benefits

One can get the virtues much higher than one thousand Ashwamedha Yagya and a hundred Rajsuya Yagya.

Aarti

Jay Pashakunsha Ekadashi-

Jay Jay Pashakunsha Ekadashi

Aso mahino chhe nyaro,

Shukla paksha e chhe pyaro

Akshay punya pame,

Sukh ne nit e paame.......

Jay Pashakunsha Ekadashi

Ekadashi ma te shreshthi,

sauthi punya ma Jyeshthi

Dhan Dhanya te deti,

purvajo no uddhar karti

Jay Jay Pashakunsha Ekadashi

Vrat Pashakunsha karjo,

antar manma preme dharjo

Falshe evu ek di jo jo jag mahe naam karsho....

Jay Jay Pashakunsha Ekadashi.

*****

24) Rama Ekadashi

<u>Rama Ekadashi- Ashwin (Aso)vad: -</u> Krishna Ekadashi / waning Ekadashi.

The significance of this Ekadashi is described by Lord Shri Krishna to the king Yudhishthir. The Lord said, "The eleventh tithi of the waning phase of Ashwin month is known as Rama Ekadashi, this tithi provides happiness and prosperity. All sins get destroyed after observing this fast."

<u>Ekadashi story</u>

Many many years ago there was a famous king named Muchkund. He was truthful, pious, a great devotee of Lord Vishnu, and regularly performed devotional services. He took care of his subjects and there was no disturbance in his Kingdom. The king's daughter 'Chandrabhaga' was named after the sacred river Chandrabhaga because the river was born as the king's daughter. She was married to a prince Shobhana, son of the king Chandrasen. Once, Prince Shobhana visited his father-in-law's palace a day before Rama Ekadashi which is on the day of Dasam tithi. That day the king struck a large kettledrum and announced "Nobody should eat on Ekadashi day." Hearing this Shobhana was surprised, he asked his wife, "Oh dear, please tell me what do I have to do now?" Chandrabagha replied, "My dear husband, In my father's Kingdom not only humans but even the pet animals observe Ekadashi fast and don't eat. If you eat you will be condemned here so you make up your mind to fast." Shobhan said, "I think you are right, I will fast tomorrow. Whatever my fate is, it will surely come to pass. "Thus, with a firm decision price Shobhana observed the fast, but due to ill health, he died early morning the next day. King Muchkund performed his cremation ceremony with a royal procession. Chandrabhaga, after performing all the purificatory processes and procedures for honoring her deceased husband (completion of after-death ceremony) continued to live in her father's house.

In his afterlife, Prince Shobhana became the ruler of a kingdom situated on the peak of Mandarachal Mountain due to the virtue of the Ekadashi fast. Gandharvas and Apsaras of that city offered him divine ornaments and a stunning crown. His personality became impressive, he became as rich and as divine as Kuber (King of wealth). Once a renowned Brahmin Som Sharma, a native of the king Muchkund's kingdom went on pilgrimage, while traveling he reached the Mandarachal Mountain. There he saw the prince Shobhan so he went closer to him. at the Same time prince, Shobhan also recognized him and immediately woke up from his seat to welcome him. He bowed down to him and asked for everyone's well-being in the kingdom and his beloved wife and father-in-law. Som Sharma replied, "Oh King Shobhan all are fine but I am astonished that, how do you become the king of such a beautiful and luxurious kingdom? I have not seen such a kingdom before!" The King said, "I had observed Rama Ekadashi Vrat when I was in your kingdom, due to the influence of those virtues I am placed here, but my Vrat was without faith and somehow with compulsion and that is why I feel that this city and its grandeur is for a temporary period. Please narrate this to my beloved wife Chandrabhaga and ask her the way to make it permanent."

Som Sharma went back to his Kingdom and narrated the whole incident and also explained in detail the glory of his Kingdom. He added, "The only problem is that the Kingdom is temporary and could vanish so he hopes you can find a way to make it permanent." Chandrabhaga who was overjoyed to hear this news about his husband said, "Oh Brahman, I am eager to see my husband, please take me there. I will make that Kingdom permanent with the influence of my virtues of the Vrats."

Chandrababu and Som Sharma went to the ashram of Vamdev Muni near Mandarachal Mountain. Therewith the power of great Rishi Vamdev Muni's chanting of hymns and her virtues which she had collected from Ekadashi Vrats her body becomes divine and with the divine flow, she reached her husband. King Shobhana was overwhelmed to see his beloved wife and made her sit on the throne left to him. Chandrabhaga said, "O dearest husband (patient), Please listen as I tell you something that will benefit you greatly. Since I was 8 years old, I have fasted regularly and with full faith in every Ekadashi. If I transfer to you all the merit, I have accumulated your kingdom will surely become permanent and its prosperity will grow and grow until the end of this Kalpa.

This way Chandrabaga became a lady with divine aura, beautiful costumes, and the finest ornament, she had an elegant personality and was enjoying life with her husband in peace and happiness.

After completing the story Lord Krishna stated to the king Yudhishthir that now you must have concluded how virtuous this Rama Ekadashi is!

Significance according to pushti Sampraday

This Ekadashi should be observed by all Vaishnavas of PushtiMarg. Everyone wishes each other for the upcoming Diwali festival celebration because all festivals start on this day. It is also said that a Vraj gopika 'Rama' wishes for the Diwali festival to Nand baba and Yashoda Maiya in their palace.

Significance According to Maryada path

According to Brahma Vaivarta Purana princess chandrabhaga, daughter of the king Muchkund was reborn as princess Satya bhama as a daughter of king Satyajit. Due to her collected virtues, she got married to Lord Shri Krishna. Once she asked for the beautiful and very romantic flowers of a heavenly tree 'Parijat'. To fulfill her wish.

Lord Shri Krishna declared war with Lord Indra and defeated him. The Lord brought that tree from heaven and planted it in his courtyard on Rama Ekadashi day.

The meaning of the word 'Bhama' (Satyabhama) is also Rama and because of that, this Ekadashi is known as Rama Ekadashi.

Offerings to Lord Vishnu

Banana fruit is supposed to be offered to Lord on this day.

Benefits

Those who observe, listen or read about this Vrat their all sins get destroyed and they attain Moksha or Vaikuntha Dham.

<u>**Aarti**</u>

Jay Jay Rama Ekadashi,

Jay Jay Rama Ekadashi

Aso mahino gatha,

krishna paksha e thai katha

Shobhan patni Rama thi,

Naam padyu taru eti

Ekadashi chhe tethi......Jay Jay Rama Ekadashi

Brahma hatya paap jaaye,

sarv sukhi thaye

Tari Aarti Gaye........Jay Jay Rama Ekadashi

Vrat Rama evu ujade,

Gaam akhu je koi gajve

Teni per Naav thase,

Samruddhi chhalka she gajve...

Jay Jay Rama Ekadashi

*****

25) Padmini Ekadashi

Padmini or Kamla Ekadashi: - Adhik month's or Purushottam month's Shukla paksha / waxing phase.

According to the Padma Purana, this Ekadashi is known as Purushottam Ekadashi, whereas in Mahabharata it is known as Samudra Ekadashi. Apart from that generally it is known as Padmini or Kamla Ekadashi. The significance of this Ekadashi is described by Lord Shri Krishna to the king Yudhishthir. Lord said the name of waxing fortnight's eleventh tithi in Adhik month is Padmini.

Those who observe fast on this day will surely attain Vaikuntha Dham. This day is very sacred, destroys all sins, and provides Moksha.

<u>**Ekadashi story**</u>

Now the incident which is narrated is about those who have faithfully observed the Padmini Ekadashi vrat, which was previously told by Rishi Pulatsya to Devarshi Narada.

Once the king Krutaveerya's (at some places you may find Kartavirya) son Sahastrarjun defeated the great king Ravana and imprisoned him. The great sage Pulastya went to the Kartavirya and requested to free Ravana and save him. On hearing this Narad Muni was surprised and asked, "Maharishi! How is it possible that the mighty and strong Ravana who also has exclusive powers can be defeated by the king Krutaveerya? Because he had conquered all Devtas and the king, Indra, too! Please explain to me that."

As an answer, the great sage narrated a story, "O Narada! Long ago there was a king named Krutaveerya. He had one hundred queens but none of his queens had a son who could rule the Kingdom. To fulfill a desire, he invited many Brahmins and did many Yagyas but it didn't work. Without a son, all luxuries and pleasures of life had no charm for him."

He started to remain unhappy. Finally, he decided to go to the forest and do Tapasya to achieve divine powers. His wife Padmini, (who was the daughter of the great truthful king Harishchandra) also followed her husband in simple clothes and without any ornaments. They both went on 'Gandhamadana mountain' and did intense Tapasya (penance) for ten thousand years. There were only bones left in the king's body, and yet, no results. Devi Padmini was a very pious and virtuous lady. She went to 'Mahasati Anusuya' and asked her the reason behind no fruition or blessing of the Lord for a son even after such a long Tapasya. Mahasati Anusuya suggested that she should observe the waxing phase Ekadashi Vrat of

Purushottam (it is also known as Mal maas) month. She also told her all the rituals of Vrat and did 'Jagran' night awakening by chanting holy names. Devi Padmini did Vrat perfectly with all rituals and true devotions towards the Lord. The Lord please to her and ask for a boon.

Devi Padmini replied, 'Oh Lord if you are really happy, please give this boon to my husband. The Lord said, "Devi Padmini, I admire the Purushottam month and its Ekadashi tithi. You have observed this Vrat with true devotion so I am very happy with you and surely fulfill your wish." Then he turned to the king and asked for a boon.

The king said, "Oh Lord, please grant me a virtuous son who is brave, kind, respectful towards all, and also can conquer the humans and demons." The Lord said 'Tathstu' and disappeared from there. The King and queen happily returned to their kingdom.

After some time, queen, Padmavati gave birth to a prince Sahastrarjun.

He became 'Chakravarti' (very brave and noble) king and defeated Ravana.

All this grace and prosperity in their kingdom was the influence of Padmini Ekadashi Vrat. After completing the story, the sage Pulastya went from there.

Views and Significance according to Pushti Sampraday

In the Purushottam maas pushti, devotees celebrate all the festivals of the year in Vaishnava temples (generally known as Haveli) and are involved with true devotions. The celebration of these festivals is known as 'Manorath.' There is also an emotion while celebrating these Manoraths that Devi Laxmi who resides in Vaikuntha is also joining Vaishnava (Vaishnavas who are like Gopa and Gopis of Vraj) to serve the Lord and enjoy eternal happiness.

Small poem (Pada) on that

Sandhya same shingar nautam,

Ful guthe sau mali

Sadan shobha Nirakhta te,

Laxmi pamya man radi,

Vaas vanchhe Vraj vseva,

eni pere sukh pamva

Shri purushottam Uttam varne,

same joi Shir Namva

Thus Laxmi Devi (also known as Devi Padmini) joins Vaishnavas for celebration, this Ekadashi is known as Padmini Ekadashi.

Significance according to Maryada Path

Long ago there was a king, he had a beautiful daughter named Padmini. She was married to king Krutaveerya of the Mahishmati kingdom. They had no heir so Brahmaharshi Narad Muni advised her to observe the Padmini Ekadashi Vrat which is on waxing fortnight's eleventh tithi of Purushottam month because Lord Vishnu admires this month the most. Muni told them to bathe with tamarind (which is created from the spit of Lord Brahma) and to do Vishnu Puja with lotus flowers. Devi Padmini observes Vrat as advised by Narad Muni and attains blessings from Lord Vishnu for the son whom they named Sahastrarjun. Later, he became 'Chakravarti' (very brave and noble) king.

<u>**Offerings to Lord Vishnu**</u>

Any seasonal fruit can be offered to the Lord on this day.

<u>**Benefits**</u>

For those who perform this Vrat, their all desires get fulfilled.

<u>**Aarti**</u>

Jay Padmini Ekadashi,

Jay Jay Padmini Ekadashi

Adik maase pragatvu,

Shukla paksha ma Sancharvu

Durbal ne Vrat karvu,

bal tene re Malvu.............

Jay Jay Padmini Ekadashi

Dashmi e Vrat Sharu karyu,

tethi mujne aaya Falyu

Sandhy tarpan kari,

prasad nu Vaasan dharyu.......

Jay Jay Padmini Ekadashi

Vrat Padmini Ujavyu Aaj Prassan tha-ya Sauna kaaj

Tane Padmini Vandan karu,

Rakhi mari te to laaj.........

Jay Jay Padmini Ekadashi

*****

26) Parama Ekadashi

Parama Ekadashi: - Adhik/Purushottam month - Krishna paksha/waning phase.

The importance of this Ekadashi is described by Lord Shri Krishna to the king Yudhishthir. The Lord said, oh king, This Ekadashi is known as 'Parama' Ekadashi.

Those who observe this Vrat their all sins get destroyed. Now listen to the beautiful story of this Ekadashi"

Ekadashi story

There lived a very pious and religious Brahmin named 'Sumedha' in the famous town named 'Kampilya' His wife was very virtuous, yet they were poor due to some accumulated sins of previous births. Yet, she always fed her husband and any guest or brahmin first and ate later. Sometimes she remained hungry also. Brahmin was aware of how difficult it is to run a house without money. So, he decided to go to another town for earnings and told his wife about that. On this, his wife said, "Oh my beloved husband, a wife should obey her husband despite right or wrong whatever he says. Everyone has to face his destiny because you can't change it and to be ready for accepting the fruition of their ' karma 'so I don't think you need to go to any other place, if it is in our destiny we will get here also."

Brahmin agreed with his wife and canceled his plans for going to another town. Once Kaundinya Muni came to his place. They both were pleased to see him. They greeted the sage with love and respect and offered food. Later they said, we are really glad to see you. Your presence will surely change our days and your guidance will help us to eradicate poverty. "The sage suggested that they should observe 'Parama' Ekadashi Vrat and said, "The virtue of that fast will destroy your sins, eradicate your poverty and solve your problems. You will be healthy and wealthy. Lord Shiva offered the post of 'king of wealth' to the Kuber and the king Harishchandra regained his kingdom and family as the result of the virtues of this Vrat." He also advised them to do 'Jagran' (night awakening) on Ekadashi night.

Brahmin and his wife observed this Vrat for five days with true devotion and completed Vrat as per rituals. The next day a young prince came to their hut and presented them with one village for daily earnings and a beautiful house to stay in.

They lived happily ever after and attained heaven after death.

<u>Views and significance according to pushti sampradaya</u>

Parama Ekadashi is describing the importance of Yamuna Maharaniji. Those who do a chant of Shri Yamunashtak (slokas on river Yamuna written by Shri Mahaprabhuji). Their all sins get destroyed and they are easily able to control the weakness of their nature. Due to her, grace Lord accepts his devotees with their innate faults and as they are. Rama means Laxmidevi and param means who provides internal happiness and joy and one who does this is Shri Yamuna Maharani.

Significance according to Maryada Path

Birth as a human is very rare because one gets it after cycling through eighty-four lakh births as other insects and animals. The way cows among all animals, Brahmin amongst humans, and the Indra among all Devtas are superior, similarly, Purushottam month is best among all months and Lord Vishnu admires it. The story of Ekadashi written above is told by Kaundinya Muni to the pious Brahmin lady named Apara. Adhik month is such a month that removes the pain and provides happiness.

Offerings to Lord Vishnu

Seasonal fruits are to be offered to the Lord on this day.

Benefits

This Ekadashi destroys sins, solves worldly problems, and removes poverty.

After observing this Vrat one becomes wealthy.

Aarti

Jay Jay Parama Ekadashi,

Jay Jay Parama Ekadashi

Purshottam maase padhare,

Krishna paksha e vistare

Jay pitambardhai,

Jay Jay Giridhari,

Jay Jay jugdadhar,

bhakt ni karje vhar...Jay Jay

Pavitra purushottam maas,

puja kare bhakt vatsal,

Puja fale jo amari,

Jo rize tu trata,

To apje amne saata jay srushti na swami....Jay...Jay

*****

Feedback

A small initiative globally for society.

**Do you know, that a tap that drips once every second
wastes about 1,000 liters of water every month.
#SAVE WATER #SAVE EARTH**

One Man NGO: Shri Aabid Surati (Painter, Author, Cartoonist, Activist)
www.ddfmumbai.org

We would be happy to have your feedback...☺

Please share your transparent review/feedback/rating to encourage our author or services. Share your testimonials by clicking the link on www.nexus-stories.com

Our books (eBook & Paperback) are available globally.
www.nexus-stories.com # Amazon # Flipkart

@nexus.stories

@nexus_stories

@Nexus Stories

@nexusstories2016

@ nexus-stories

Have a Happy Reading...!!! ☺